Losing Louis

Simon Mendes da Costa's first play, *Table for One*, was performed at the Hen and Chickens Theatre, Islington, in November 2001 (*Time Out*'s critic's choice). *Losing Louis* is his second staged play. He is currently working on his third play and a project for television.

T0258343

Simon Mendes da Costa

Losing Louis

Methuen Drama

Published by Methuen Drama

3 5 7 9 10 8 6 4 2

First published in 2005 by
Methuen Publishing Limited

Methuen Drama
A & C Black Publishers Limited
38 Soho Square
London W1D 3HB

A CIP catalogue record for this book is available
from the British Library

ISBN 978 0 413 77512 2

Typeset by Country Setting, Kingsdown, Kent

Losing Louis

For Grandma,
a pure diamond

To Michael, Robin
and my dear Saffron, with thanks.
And in fond memory of Rod

The world premiere of *Losing Louis* was presented by arrangement with Michael Codron at the Hampstead Theatre, London, on 24 January, 2005. The cast was as follows:

Bella Holland	Anita Briem
Louis Judah Ellis	Jason Durr
Tony Ellis	David Horovitch
Sheila Ellis	Alison Steadman
Bobbie Ellis	Emma Cunniffe
Elizabeth Ellis	Lynda Bellingham
Reggie Ellis	Brian Protheroe

Directed by	Robin Lefèvre
Designed by	Liz Ascroft
Lighting by	Mick Hughes

The playscript that follows was correct at the start of rehearsals, but may have changed during the rehearsal process.

Characters

Bella Holland, *early twenties*
Louis Judah Ellis, *late twenties / early thirties*
Tony Ellis, *fifties*
Sheila Ellis, *fifties*
Bobbie Ellis, *late twenties*
Elizabeth Ellis, *early fifties*
Reggie Ellis, *late forties / early fifties*

All scenes take place in one large bedroom. Two doors lead from this room, one to the landing and the rest of the house and the other to an en-suite bathroom. In the room there is at least a bed, a dressing table, a mirror and a large wardrobe. There are two paintings hanging up, both in prominent positions, one is that of a young man and the other of a young woman. The action moves between past and present, all transitions between the two should be continuous and seamless.

Act One

Scene One

The past.

Lights up on **Bella** *and* **Louis** *in bed. They are fooling around.*

Bella What was that?

Louis What?

Bella I thought I heard something.

Louis Where?

Bella I'm not sure.

Louis I can't hear anything.

Bella Neither can I now.

Louis Is the door locked?

Bella Yes.

Louis It'll be the wind or maybe it's the ghost.

Bella Oh don't, Louis.

Louis Werrrrrrrr . . .

Bella Arr! Stop it . . . I definitely heard something.

Louis *disappears under the bedcovers.*

Louis Perhaps it came from under here.

Bella No, I think it came . . . What are you doing? Stop that. I've told you you mustn't do that. Mmmm. It's rude.

Louis I like it.

Bella Stop it. Come back up. Stop it. Just stop it. There it is again, something scratching.

Louis *emerges.*

Louis It's probably a mouse.

Bella A mouse!? Where?

Louis (*sings from 'A Windmill in Old Amsterdam'*) 'There on the stair, right there . . .'

Louis *disappears under the covers once more.*

Bella Ahhh. Stop it.

Louis (*sings*) 'A little mouse with clogs on, going clip-clippety-clop on the stair.'

Bella Oh yeah. Oh. No, stop that. I've told you, it's not right. I hate mice. There it is again. Listen. It's coming from under the bed.

Louis I know!

Bella Oh. Yes. That's nice. No, stop.

Louis If you insist.

Bella In a minute. Ah. Oh. Yes, just there, that's it, oh gosh, that's nice. Ah. Ah. Oh. Not so hard. Gently. Gently. Oh. Yes. Yes. That's wonderful. Crikey. Ah. Ah. That's it. Yes, that's it . . . Ah. Oh.

A toy car comes out from under the bed.

Argggh. Stop!

Louis Mmm.

Bella No, I mean it this time, I really mean it. Look, Louis, look!

Louis What?

Bella Look. A toy car.

Louis Oh God. Ssh . . . Anthony? . . . Anthony? . . . Are you under there? . . . Anthony, are you under there? Quick. Go now. Go.

Bella But . . .

Louis Go.

Bella *runs into the bathroom. As* **Louis** *talks to* **Tony** *he tidies the bed and gets dressed as best he can.*

Louis   Anthony. What are you doing under there? How many times have I told you not . . .? Daddy's not cross. We were just playing a little game. Now come out. Come out. Look, Anthony, we mustn't tell Mummy about this . . . Because it's a secret. Look at me. It's like Mummy sometimes gets cross with Tony. You don't mean to be naughty but Mummy gets cross anyway. Sometimes Mummy doesn't understand. It's the same for Daddy. You don't want Mummy to be cross, do you? So this is a special secret for us. Do you understand? Anthony, look at me. Do you understand? . . . Good. And then maybe if you're a really good boy, for your birthday, we will get you that big boy's bicycle we saw in the shops last week. Would you like that? . . . Good. Now do as you're told and come out. Come on, come with me. Come along. (**Louis** *exits, leaving the door open.*) Come on. Anthony.

Scene Two

The present.

A balding, middle-aged man enters from the bathroom. He is wearing black trousers and a white shirt, as yet no tie. He carries an overnight bag.

Sheila (*offstage*)   Tony.

Tony   Yes.

Sheila (*offstage*)   Tony.

Tony   Yes.

Sheila (*offstage*)   Anthony.

Tony   What?

Sheila (*offstage*)   Doesn't matter, I've found it.

Tony *takes out two bottles of whisky from his bag. He opens one and pours himself a large glass, then hides both bottles somewhere suitable in the room.*

Tony How long you gonna be?

Sheila (*offstage*) What?

Tony How long you gonna be?

Sheila (*offstage*) What?

Tony Forget it.

Sheila *appears from the bathroom. She is wearing a short black dress.*

Sheila What did you say?

Tony Nothing.

Sheila You've not started already? . . . Do me up, will you?

Tony Are you going out like that?

Sheila Like what?

Tony Like a prostitute.

Sheila Thank you very much. I want to look nice.

Tony Who for?

Sheila For your dad, silly.

Tony He's hardly gonna notice.

Sheila He's always liked me to look nice.

Tony I know.

Sheila Don't say it like that.

Sheila *gets her bag, then sits on the bed and does her make-up.* **Tony** *looks out of the window.*

Tony It's raining again. This must be the worst summer on record. Did you pack our wellies?

Sheila If you think I'm wearing wellington boots with this dress you've . . .

Tony There's a car coming! Oh no, it's turned off. (*He paces. He then picks up the phone, briefly listens into the receiver, replaces the handset and then immediately picks it back up again.*) Hello? Oh, sorry, Nina, Sorry. Do you think you could . . .? No, it's OK, sorry. Sorry about that. (*He replaces the handset.*) She's supposed to do what we tell her to do.

Sheila You didn't tell her to do anything. Who d'you want to ring, anyway?

Tony Thought I'd call Claire.

Sheila Don't know why you don't buy yourself a mobile like everyone else.

Tony Waste of money.

Tony *paces. He picks up a dumbbell that is in his bag on the floor and starts doing arm exercises.*

Sheila And I don't know what possessed you to bring those.

Tony I'm supposed to do it every day. That's what it said on the instructions.

Sheila I'm sure you could have missed one day.

Tony It's all about perseverance. Feel that.

Tony *makes her feel his biceps.*

Sheila Yes. Very good.

Tony Six weeks. Not bad. No one's going to kick sand in my face.

Sheila No, 'cause it's always pebbles where we go.

Tony Use both your hands and see if you can take me.

Tony *kneels down and attempts to draw her into an arm-wrestling competition.*

Sheila I'm doing my make-up.

Tony *goes back to looking out of the window. He hums a few bars of* '*A Windmill in Old Amsterdam*'.

Sheila Do you know I've just found out that we're not compatible?

Tony Really.

Sheila There's this new person who's just started at work, Freda, and she does horoscopes.

Tony Oh God.

Sheila No. No. Not the silly ones in the paper. Proper ones. You have to give her your exact time and place of birth and she can work out who you are and who you fit with.

Tony Mmm.

Sheila Anyway, I gave her you and me and she did both our charts. And it turns out your Saturn's square to my Venus.

Tony Is it?

Sheila And that's really bad. In fact she said in all her twenty years of doing it we were the least compatible couple she'd ever come across.

Tony Another car.

Sheila And I think she's right.

Tony Do you?

Sheila Yes.

Tony No, that's turned off too.

Sheila I mean, you never want to go on holiday and I always do. You don't even have a passport. You love football and I hate it. You're miserable and I'm happy.

Tony I'm not miserable.

Sheila I want to better myself and you're just happy as you are.

Tony Hah! Then I'm happy.

Sheila I've decided to take up astronomy.

Tony Oh please, not another thing.

Sheila Did you know light travels at one hundred and eighty-six thousand miles per second?

Tony No.

Sheila And the sun is ninety-three million miles from the Earth. Which means we don't see the sun now, but as it was eight minutes ago. And therefore also, because of the time it takes for light to travel from you to me, it must mean that I see you in the past.

Tony Do I have hair?

Sheila And the further you move away the more you're in the past, but the faster you move away the younger you get. But the heavier and more squashed you become. That's Einstein's theory, that is.

Tony I need another drink.

Sheila Oh shit, my lipstick's slipped down the back of the bed. Get it out for me.

Tony NO!

Sheila All right, I only asked.

Tony Why can't you?

Sheila It's filthy under there.

Tony It's all right for me to get dirty then, is it?

Sheila Go on.

Tony Wear another colour.

Sheila *gets down on all fours and attempts to retrieve her lipstick.*

Sheila   I can't, it's the only one that goes with my nails. Where are you going?

Tony   To see if they've arrived.

Sheila   What again? Are there any other cars out there?

Tony   No.

Sheila   You think they've hiked here?

Tony   Hiked? Reggie? Not without sherpas.

Sheila   I can't reach it . . . It's filthy under there. Look, I'm all messed up now. Doesn't Nina ever clean?

Sheila *goes back into the bathroom.*

Tony   Give her a break, she's almost dead. He might have parked up round the back.

Tony *exits leaving the door open.*

Scene Three

The past.

Bella *enters from the bathroom.* **Louis** *enters from the landing.*

Louis   (*to* **Tony**, *offstage*) Yes I'll be down in a minute, now run along. Off you go. (*He closes the door.*) He'll be all right.

Bella   Oh, Louis.

Louis   It'll be fine.

Bella   Oh, Louis.

Louis   Everything will be fine. Everything will be just fine. Oh, Bella.

Bella   Louis.

They hug.

What are we going to do?

Louis   We must stay calm.

Bella   He'll tell her, I know he will.

Louis   No, he won't.

Bella   He's only five.

Louis   He's very nearly six.

Bella   He adores her.

Louis   But he's scared of me.

Bella   So he won't say anything, will he?

Louis   No.

Bella   But if he does, what do we do?

Louis   We deny everything, he lives in a fantasy world. She won't believe him.

Bella   But what if she does? What do we do?

Louis   I love you, you know that, don't you?

Bella   More than Paris loves Helen?

Louis   More than Rhett loves Scarlett.

Bella   More than Apollo loves Daphne?

Louis   More than Heathcliff loves Cathy.

Bella   More than Louis loves his wife?

Louis   More.

Bella   Would you ever leave her?

Louis   Do you want me to?

Bella   We can't carry on like this.

Louis   Do you want it to stop?

Bella   No. Do you?

Louis   No. Never.

Bella   Never?

Louis   Never.

Bella   Think about this, Louis. Think about it very hard. This is very important. Do you really, truly love me?

Louis   I've never truly loved anyone else.

Bella   I think I might be pregnant.

Bobbie (*offstage*)   Lou-lou. Where are you?

Louis   Oh God. Um. Just coming, Bobbie. Quick. Go back to your room. We'll talk about this later.

Bobbie (*offstage*)   Lou-lou.

Louis   Just coming, Bobbie. Oh Bella, I love you. Just coming.

Bella *and* **Louis** *exit.*

Scene Four

The present.

Sheila *enters from the bathroom and looks out of the window.* **Tony** *enters from the landing.*

Tony   I really don't know why Nina had to put us in here.

Sheila   And have they?

Tony   What?

Sheila   Arrived.

Tony   Not yet.

Sheila   Really.

Tony   I wonder what he's driving these days?

Sheila   A car, maybe.

Tony   Not just any car. Not our little Reggie. It'll probably be a Merc or a Jag or a Porsche or maybe even a Lamborghini . . . or a Ferrari. Or a Maclaren F1 . . . Can you imagine anyone spending over half a million quid on a car?

Sheila   Not in Crawley.

Tony *pours himself another drink.*

Sheila   Tony!

Tony   What?

Sheila   Go easy on that, you've got to make a speech.

Tony   It's not a speech, it's a eulogy.

Sheila   Whatever.

Tony   Don't worry. I'll have to stand up and say nice things so they'll expect me to be drunk. You want one?

Sheila   No. Will Reggie be making a . . . eulogy?

Tony *(laughs)* No. Reggie'll be making a speech. And there won't be a dry eye in the house.

Sheila   He has a way with words, does your brother.

Tony   Which has kept many a guilty man walking the streets. The prison service must love him.

Sheila   Ciggy?

Tony   No. We've got to sleep in here.

Sheila   I won't go on about your drinking if you for once just belt up about my smoking.

Tony   I wonder if he's still got all his hair?

Sheila   Does your hair fall out when you die?

Tony   Not Dad, you idiot – Reggie. I bet he has.

Sheila   He had a good head of hair, did Reggie. Ended up with your mum's good looks and your dad's brains. Bit ironic, isn't it?

Tony   Oh, I don't begrudge him that, why should I? I mean, I don't begrudge him his private schooling, I know they could only afford state education when I was young. Or the extra tuition so he could get a place at Oxford, I don't begrudge him that. I don't begrudge the fact that he could never do anything wrong, that would be unfair of me. I don't begrudge that Dad took him to the FA Cup Final and left me at home.

Sheila   Oh God.

Tony   The thing is, all I ever wanted . . .

Sheila   . . . was a drum kit. I know.

Tony   No. I wasn't going to say drum kit. I wasn't.

Sheila   What were you going to say, then?

Tony   I can't remember . . . I did have rhythm though. I still do . . . But oh no, I couldn't have one, could I, nowhere to play it. Buddy Rich was . . .

Sheila   Oh, sod Buddy Rich.

Tony   He was already being featured in his parent's vaudeville act at the age of eighteen months and he had his own solo drumming spot by the age of six. You need support and you need to start young.

Sheila   Yeah, yeah.

Tony   Give us a puff.

Tony *takes a puff of her cigarette and* **Sheila** *takes a swig of his drink.*

Sheila   How do I look?

Tony   I've already told you.

Sheila   You never did understand clothes.

Tony   What's there to understand?

Sheila   Exactly. Reggie was always nicely turned out.
Anyway, it'll be nice to see the lovely Lissie again, won't it?

Tony   Mmm.

Sheila   Nice nice or just nice.

Tony   Don't be disgusting.

Sheila   I expect she's aged badly. I always thought she'd go
to seed. Didn't you?

Tony   No. Not really.

Sheila   She was that type. You can always tell. And are
their wonderful children coming?

Tony   Oh no. God spare us that. God spare us the twins.

Sheila   Yes. God spare us the twins. Perfect children.

Tony   For the perfect couple. Mr and Mrs Perfect.

Sheila   The Perfects.

Tony   Yes. The Perfects. We should have brought Claire.

Sheila   Let's not start that again.

Tony   She's missing her day out.

Sheila   It's a funeral. She's better where she is.

Tony   That's what you always say. She'll wonder what's
happened.

Sheila   You rang them, didn't you?

Tony   Yes, I did.

Sheila   Well, there you go.

Tony   But she'll be confused. She gets confused. She looks
forward to her football. Why did he have to be buried on a
Saturday?

Sheila   You arranged it.

Tony   Well, I could hardly organise it before Reggie could deign to get back, could I?

Sheila   Are you allowed to be buried on a Saturday?

Tony   Why not?

Sheila   Because it's the sabbath . . . And at a church?

Tony   He wasn't bothered about all that stuff. (*He looks at the painting of his father.*) Died peacefully in his sleep, it hardly seems right, does it?

Sheila   Oh, I almost forgot. (*She gets a small package out of her handbag and gives it to* **Tony**.) Happy birthday.

Tony   Thank you. What is it?

Sheila   Open it and see.

Tony *opens the present: it is a very brightly coloured tie.*

Tony (*genuinely*) Thank you. It's lovely. I really like that.

Sheila   And I bought you a cake, it's only small, but it's the thought that counts.

Sheila *hands him an individual cake.*

Tony   Thank you.

Sheila   There's a new coffee-shop opened up in the village, I got it while you were getting petrol.

Tony   Mmm. It's good.

Sheila   Well, go on then, try it on.

Tony   This is really very good.

Sheila   Try it on.

Tony   Today? I don't think he'd approve.

Sheila   He'll never know . . . Oh my God!

Tony   What?

Sheila Died peacefully in his sleep, you said.

Tony Yes.

Sheila He didn't . . . you know . . . die there, did he?

Tony Don't worry. I'm sure they've changed the sheets.

Sheila Arggh! No! Really. What about the mattress?

Tony It's got a rubber undersheet.

Sheila Urggh. No. I am not sleeping there.

Tony *refers to the two paintings.*

Tony Look at the two of them. Both trying to figure the other out. You know, I always thought this was Mum. That's him, but this isn't her. I always thought it was, though, but it's just a painting he picked up somewhere.

Sheila It's nothing like her.

Tony It is. Anyway, when you're six things get blurred.

Sheila They'll be getting blurred now if you carry on knocking that stuff back. Come on, let's get out of here. I feel quite sick.

Tony It's more like her than any picture I've ever seen.

Sheila Really.

Tony Captures her spirit.

Sheila It's horrible. Come on, get your stuff.

Tony There used to be a light above it.

Sheila Really.

Tony You know, one of those special picture strip lights, but they took it out, don't know why. It had a big thick electricity wire running from it, to behind the picture. Stopped it hanging flush to the wall.

Sheila   Tony, this is fascinating, but I'm finding all this just a bit creepy.

Tony   And behind the picture it went straight into the wall and came out in my room next door.

Sheila   Are you planning on showing me a wiring diagram?

Tony   Some gimcrack builder's bodge job, I imagine.

Sheila   God, I could listen to you for hours.

Tony   There is a point to this.

Sheila   Well, hurry up and get to it because I can't get the image of your decaying father out of my mind.

Tony   What I'm saying is that as a child, as a six-year-old child, I was obsessed with this room. It was the one place I wasn't allowed to go.

Sheila   Looks like I better sit down for this. (*She goes to sit on the bed, then changes her mind and sits on the chair.*) Woarrgh!

Tony   And when they took that light out they pulled the wire out too, which left a hole right through into my room. If you take that picture down now I bet it's still there.

Sheila   Ciggy?

Tony   Are you listening to me?

Sheila   Give me another option.

Tony   Not today, no. Let's see. (*He takes the picture down and props it against the wall. A hole is exposed.*) There you go. Typical of the old man, if you can't see it, it doesn't need dealing with.

Sheila   Bit like your penis.

Tony   That's not even funny.

Sheila   I know.

Tony   Or accurate.

Sheila Just trying to lighten the mood.

Tony I'm burying my father today.

Sheila Where are you going?

Tony I want to see if you can still see through into here.

Sheila You dirty little pervert.

Tony I'm not a pervert.

Sheila You played peek-a-boo into your parents' bedroom.

Tony Just the once, on my sixth birthday, after that I never wanted to again.

Tony *exits.*

Sheila Well, don't leave me here on my own.

Sheila *exits, leaving the door open.*

Scene Five

The past.

Bobbie *enters from the bathroom, she is heavily pregnant. She makes her way across to the bed and lies down. She puts a pillow under her feet, lays a flannel across her head then lights a cigarette.* **Louis** *enters pushing a brand new red child's bicycle.* **Bobbie** *makes herself more attractive.*

Louis Where is he?

Bobbie Don't bring that it in here, Lou-lou. It'll get my carpets all dirty.

Louis It's brand new.

Louis *leaves the bicycle in the middle of the room.* **Bobbie** *gets up off the bed, takes* **Louis'** *jacket off for him, then hangs it up.*

Louis Where is he?

Bobbie In his room.

Louis   On his birthday? What's the painting doing down?

Bobbie   Tony wanted to have a closer look at it.

Louis   I'm worried about that boy.

Louis *makes to exit.*

Bobbie   Lou-lou. Haven't you forgotten something?

Louis   What?

Bobbie   A kiss for your Bobbie.

Louis *kisses* **Bobbie**.

Bobbie   Where's Bella?

Louis   In her room, I think.

Bobbie   Ask her to come in here, will you?

Louis   Why?

Bobbie   Because I need her. Don't be so grouchy. What's made my Lou-lou so grouchy?

Louis   (*calling from the door*) Bella! Bobbie wants you.

Bobbie   Lou-lou, perhaps it's about time Bella moved out.

Louis   Why? Won't you need her help?

Bobbie   Well, there's always Nina.

Louis   We won't be able to afford to keep Nina on, not without the money Bella gives us. I know it's not much, but she needs an affordable place, otherwise she won't be able to continue with her studying. She's going to be an excellent solicitor, everyone at the office agrees. We have to give her some more time.

Bobbie   Yes I know, but . . .

Louis   Look, I promised her father and I never go back on my word.

Louis *exits.*

Bobbie   Yes. Sorry, Lou-lou. Yes, of course. Sorry.

Bobbie *returns to her pose of suffering on the bed.* **Bella** *enters.*

Bobbie Oh Bella! Bella! Thank God! I need you.

Bella Why?

Bobbie It's my feet, and my head, oh, and my back too, but mainly it's my feet. Look at my ankles, they're the size of tree-trunks.

Bella Hardly.

Bobbie Will they ever go back to normal? And my veins are just popping out everywhere. Louis will never look at me again.

Bella Don't be silly.

Bobbie Make Bobbie feel better. Please. Pleeease.

Bella Go on then, give them here.

Bobbie You are a poppet. What I'd do without you I do not know.

Bella You'd do fine.

Bobbie Oh, I'm not so sure. Oh Bella, that's so good. You've got wonderful hands. I bet you make your Tom a very happy man.

Bella Bobbie!

Bobbie When's he back off leave?

Bella Next week.

Bobbie I imagine he can't wait to whip you down the aisle.

Bella I'm don't want to be an army wife.

Bobbie I know what you mean, that's why I made Louis leave the Navy, but Tom's an officer – that's different.

Bella Anyway he's not Jewish.

Bobbie Neither was I, but it's quite easy to change. All I had to do was go with these nice women, they dunked me in a bath and then cut my nails. Easy.

Bella   I need to finish my articles first. There's more to life than having a husband.

Bobbie   You're so modern. But I like the fact you're playing hard to get. I played hard to get. For about a week. Louis's not a patient man. I like Tom, he's very funny. Men like Tom don't come along every day.

Bella   No.

Bobbie   Get yourself pregnant, that always works.

Bella   Bobbie!

Bobbie   Worked for me . . . Arggh.

Bella   Sorry, did that hurt?

Bobbie   No. It was the baby. Ow. He can't wait to get out, can he?

Bella   It's a he, is it?

Bobbie   I don't know if Louis would be able to cope with a girl. He says Tony's turning into such a big sissy, it'd better be a boy to even things up.

Bella   And what names are you considering this week?

Bobbie   Oh, we've decided, I thought Louis would have told you.

Bella   No.

Bobbie   If it's a boy, we're going to name him Reggie.

Bella   So you got your way, then.

Bobbie   Louis wanted to call him Judah.

Bella   My uncle's called Judah.

Bobbie   Well, it may be a good Jewish name, but I'm buggered if I'm calling him that.

Bella   Bobbie, you are a card.

Bobbie   And Tony wanted to call him Erastus after a boy at his school. But that's a darky name though, isn't it? I just love Reggie. Reggie, Reggie, Reggie, Reggie, Reggie. Ooo, you can almost eat it.

Bella   And if it's a girl?

Bobbie   It doesn't feel like a girl, not today anyway, but secretly I hope it is. You can do so much more with girls. You can dress them up. Boys don't like being dressed up. Though the other day I caught Tony trying on one of my outfits.

Bella   Did you?

Bobbie   The gold evening gown.

Bella   Well, at least he shows taste.

Bobbie   Louis was furious.

Bella   I bet he was.

Bobbie   And also girls can come shopping with you and tell you all about their boyfriends.

Bella   I never told my parents about mine.

Bobbie   I did. I told them everything. There were no secrets in our family.

Bella   So if it is, what are you going to call her?

Bobbie   You're going to love this. Because Louis and I agree on this one. We're going to call her after you.

Bella   No!

Bobbie   Isabella.

Bella   You can't.

Bobbie   It's such a lovely name. I wish you didn't shorten it. But in a way I'm glad you do, because it's like a different name but the same as well. Do you see?

Bella   Yes.

Bobbie   And it's just our way of saying thank you. For all you've done.

Bella   I'm just repaying your generosity.

Bobbie   But we're friends now, aren't we?

Bella   Of course we are.

Bobbie   Best friends. Would you say we're best friends?

Bella   Of course.

Bobbie   We're like real Jewish sisters. Of course you're the clever one. Like my Louis. He's clever. He's brilliant. I'm glad I'm not clever.

Bella   Why not? I mean you are.

Bobbie   I'm not. I'm a bit stupid, really.

Bella   You're not stupid.

Bobbie   I feel stupid. I don't know as much as other people. They all laugh at things I don't understand. I watch you and Louis some nights chattering away about this and that and, well, I just watch . . . I don't know what would have become of me without Louis. I wasn't cut out to be poor. I don't want you to leave, I need you, you know that.

Bella   Why would I leave?

Bobbie   Promise me you won't.

Bella   Well . . .

Bobbie   Not for ever of course, but not while I'm like this. Wait until I'm back to my old self again. Promise me that.

Bella   Um.

Bobbie   Promise me.

Bella   I promise.

Bobbie   Good, that's settled.

Louis *enters, carrying a model ship.*

Bobbie   I've seen your father play cards on the Sabbath whilst eating a bacon sandwich. Is that tradition? No. Tradition or not, I don't like it. He was a lovely baby until they went and did that. Smiled at everyone, go to anyone. Then those men came and . . . ugh, makes me shudder to think of it. Screamed for hours. Poor little mite. And the blood, you never said there was going to be blood. Didn't seem big enough to have a bit cut off it.

Louis   It'll get bigger.

Bobbie   It's like he became a different baby overnight. His whole personality changed.

Louis   It's not down to that.

Bobbie   I'm not so sure. He still doesn't like men.

Louis   He's not been wearing any of your clothes again, has he?

Bobbie   No.

Louis   Good.

Bobbie   What's that you've got there?

Louis   A ship. A model ship.

Bobbie   As well?

Louis   It's a replica of the one I served on during my National Service.

Bobbie   You're spoiling him this year.

Louis   I'm just delighted for once that he's showing an interest in normal things.

Louis *sits on the bed,* **Bobbie** *gets up and removes his shoes. She gets a sharp pain in her stomach.*

Bobbie   Ooo. Ow. I'll be glad when this is all over . . . Can I fetch you anything?

Louis   No.

Bobbie Did you have a good day?

Louis No.

Bobbie *starts to remove* **Louis'** *belt and undo his trousers.*

Bobbie Oh dear.

Louis It's that bloody Burton case.

Bobbie Bloody Burton people.

Louis I just don't know why they won't settle. Surely anyone can see the evidence is against them.

Bobbie Yes.

Louis They've practically admitted liability anyway, off the record. But no prejudice is no prejudice. Sometimes I think that . . . What are you doing?

Bobbie Just helping you relax.

Louis Well, don't.

Bobbie I want to make you feel better.

Louis I feel fine.

Bobbie I'm worried about you. I'm worried that you're missing out. What with me being like this. I don't want you to miss out.

Louis I'm not missing out.

Bobbie Aren't you?

Louis Well, yes, I am, but no. Oh, go on then. But be quick, I want to give Tony his present.

There is a knock on the bedroom door.

Louis Come in.

Bella *enters, carrying a glass of iced tea.*

Bella Sorry to. disturb you. I promised I'd tell you. Tony asks if he can come out of his room now. He says he's very sorry and he wants to ride on his new bicycle.

Bobbie   He can come out at six, not before.

Bella   Six? I'll tell him. Louis would you like tea?

Louis   No, thank you.

Bobbie   I'll take mine downstairs.

Bella *exits taking the tea with her.* **Bobbie** *goes to follow her.*

Louis   What's he done?

Bobbie   Nothing.

Louis   What's he done?

Bobbie   Oh, you know children.

Louis   Bobbie, what's he done?

Bobbie   How did he know he was getting a bicycle?

Louis   Bobbie?

Bobbie   I had to smack him, that's all.

Louis   What's he been doing?

Bobbie   Louis, let me do this for you. It'll make you feel better.

Louis   Tell me.

Bobbie   No, it's horrible. Horrible lies. Let's forget all about it and relax.

Louis   Forget about what? Get off me. What lies?

Bobbie   I expect he got muddled that's all. He's only six.

Louis   Old enough to know right from wrong. What's he been saying?

Bobbie   I can't tell you. Lie down, please . . .

Louis   Get off.

Bobbie   Please, Louis, please. You'll feel better.

Louis   What's he been saying?

Bobbie   It's not true, I know that.

Louis   What?

Bobbie   Silly. About you and Bella.

Louis   About me and Bella?

Bobbie   Yes, but I know it's not true. I know it's not true.
I know that. So let's not say any more about it. Please,
Louis, just lie down.

Louis   What did he say?

Bobbie   Nothing.

Louis   I'll put the strap across him, birthday or no
birthday.

Bobbie   No, Louis, no.

Louis *picks up the bike and puts it in the wardrobe along with the
model ship.*

Bobbie   He got confused. He was very upset. Probably got
mixed up with a dream. I know it's not true. Don't leave
me, will you?

Louis   What?

Bobbie   I know I'm all fat and ugly and you probably hate
me. I wouldn't blame you if you did. Bella's beautiful.

Louis   Shut up.

Bobbie   And clever. She's very clever.

Louis   Shut up.

Bobbie   I like her so much.

Louis   Shut up.

Bobbie   I don't blame you. I'm ugly and fat, but soon I'll
be back to my old self. (*She feels the baby coming.*) Louis . . .
Oh Louis . . . The baby's coming.

Louis   Oh. I'll fetch Bella. Bella! Bella!

Bobbie   No, I'm fine. Don't worry about me. I'll be fine.

Louis   What should I do?

Bobbie   Get Bella, Louis, get Bella.

Louis   Bella! Where is she?

Bobbie   Louis.

Louis   Yes?

Bobbie   I'm scared.

Louis   Don't worry. Lou-lou's here.

Bobbie   Do you still love me?

Louis   Of course. I think we should go to the hospital now.

Bobbie   I can still do this for you, before we go.

Louis   No, Bobbie.

Bobbie   I don't mind. I like to please you.

Louis   I know you do. Bella! Come on.

Bobbie   I don't want it to hurt so much this time.

Louis   It won't.

Bobbie   Promise.

Louis   I promise.

Louis *helps* **Bobbie** *out of the room. They leave the door open.*

Scene Six

The present.

Tony *and* **Sheila** *enter.* **Sheila** *busies herself with packing their stuff up. During the scene* **Tony** *puts the painting back on its hook.*

Tony   I really upset her and then she slapped me round the face.

Sheila On your birthday?

Tony And so I was sent to my room.

Sheila On your birthday?

Tony So I spied on them through the hole. And that's when I saw the bike. But then they all went out and left me.

Sheila On your birthday?

Tony You sound like a parrot. On your birthday. On your birthday. On your birthday. That's hardly the point, is it?

Sheila Isn't it?

Tony No.

Sheila Well, what is then? . . . Where did they go?

Tony Just out.

Sheila On your . . . They left you in the house alone.

Tony Well, Nina was around. I heard her clanking about in the kitchen. Singing. She was always singing. Bella said I could come out when I heard the big clock in the hall strike six.

Sheila That clock has such a lovely chime.

Tony Let's bury him first, eh?

Sheila I just know how quickly the good stuff gets snapped up . . . Sorry. Go on.

Tony So, anyway, I heard the clock and came out and I crept in here. I took the bike out of the wardrobe and rode it round and round the room.

Sheila Is this yours?

Sheila *has picked up a hairbrush.*

Tony No.

Sheila Urggh.

Sheila *drops the hairbrush in disgust.*

Tony I'm trying to tell you something here.

Sheila I thought you'd finished.

Tony That was the only time I got to . . .

Tony *tails off.*

Sheila What? Got what?

Tony Nothing.

Sheila You're like a leaky tap.

Pause.

Tony I think I must have –

Sheila Oh God.

Tony – fallen asleep on the bed because the next thing I remember is hearing the old man coming up the stairs. I panicked. I had nowhere to go so I put the bike back and had to get in the wardrobe with it.

Sheila Good.

Tony Good?

Sheila There's a car coming.

Tony What?

Sheila Big car. Look.

Tony Where?

Sheila There. You'll see it in a moment as it comes past the . . . There! By the farm. On the Old Ford Road. See.

Tony *takes some binoculars out of his bag and looks.*

Tony Oh yes. Told you. Jag. Latest model. Typical. That's him.

Sheila You think?

Tony I know it's him, I can sense it.

Sheila How d'you feel?

Tony I don't know. I feel . . . I feel like . . .

Sheila Darth Vader? When he's on the Death Star and he senses Obi-Wan Kenobi's presence.

Tony Is everything a joke to you today?

Sheila (*as Darth Vader*) Come over to the dark side, Luke.

Tony Look at the way he came round that bend! That's very dangerous on these lanes. What happens if there's someone coming the other way?

Sheila Let go, Luke, let go. The force is strong in this one.

Tony Nip down and tell Nina we're changing rooms.

Sheila Why can't you?

Tony Look, just for once . . .

Sheila (*as Obi-Wan Kenobi*) Strike me down and I will become more powerful than ever . . . All right. I'm going.

Sheila *exits downstairs. He goes over to the wardrobe and opens the door, he then steps inside. The wardrobe door closes. The bedroom door opens and* −

Scene Seven

The past.

Louis *enters from the hall.* **Louis** *pours himself a drink and lights a cigar. He sits down in the chair.* **Bella** *enters.*

Bella Louis. What are you doing sitting here in the dark?

Louis Where have you been?

Bella I went for a walk. It's such a lovely evening.

Louis Yes.

Bella I watched the sun set up at Pitcher's Point. I needed to go up to our place and do a bit of thinking.

Louis Yes.

Bella I've been to the doctor's and I am definitely pregnant.

Louis *laughs*.

Bella Please don't laugh. I'm having your baby.

Louis She knows about us. She says she doesn't but she does. Mummy's boy Anthony didn't keep his little secret.

Bella Oh no.

Louis I could wring his neck.

Bella Oh my God . . . Where is she?

Louis Hospital.

Bella Why? What's happened?

Louis The baby came.

Bella So soon?

Louis I think the shock brought it on.

Bella I should have been here.

Louis Yes.

Bella How is she?

Louis I haven't seen her.

Bella Why not?

Louis I haven't summoned up the courage . . . The baby's dead.

Bella What?

Louis Yes, she died . . . Little girl . . . Isabella. Born dead. They don't know why.

Bella Oh, Louis.

Louis There she is, all on her own in the hospital room. No one around her, no one to talk to, and here I am sitting drinking whisky and smoking the cigar I put aside for this moment. Do you know what my first thoughts were when I heard? 'Your wife's fine, but the baby, the baby didn't live.' 'Didn't live,' that's what they said. All I wanted to do was to come here and see you. Not her. See you. She's all on her own. She knows about us, Bella. I know she knows.

Bella Come on.

Louis No.

Bella You must.

Louis I can't.

Bella Come on. She needs us now. We have to do the right thing.

Louis Do we?

Bella Yes. Come on.

Bella *helps* **Louis** *out of his chair. He collapses in her arms. Their embrace becomes more urgent and he starts to kiss her passionately. She gently breaks it off.*

Bella Come on.

Louis *and* **Bella** *exit.*

Scene Eight

The present.

The wardrobe door opens and **Tony** *comes out.*

Sheila (*offstage, shouting down the stairs*) No, don't worry, Nina, I'll do it . . . I'll do it. (*She comes in with some sheets over her arm.*) Deaf as a post, that woman.

Tony She always was, that's why I spent the night in the wardrobe.

Sheila She gave me a very funny look when I told her we were swapping rooms. She said it was all right with her, if it was all right with us. They've arrived.

Tony Did you see them?

Sheila No.

Tony I have a very bad feeling about all this.

Tony *goes into the bathroom to collect his washbag.*

Sheila You haven't seen him in ten years, maybe he's changed.

Sheila *exits.*

Tony Maybe he has. We can but hope, I suppose. Maybe he's developed an embarrassing stutter. And he's shrunk and lost all his hair.

Elizabeth *enters, carrying a dress-hanger. She is beautiful.*

Tony Hopefully he'll have pock-marked saggy skin and a big fat pot belly. False teeth, bad breath and glasses. Hardly be able to convince a jury then, would he? (*He comes out of the bathroom.*) Imagine his closing remarks . . . Arggh . . . Elizabeth.

Elizabeth Tony.

Tony God. Elizabeth. God. Yes. God, you look . . . God. Hello.

Elizabeth Hello, Tony. How are you?

Tony Fine. Yes. Fine. Yes, I'm fine.

Elizabeth Good.

Tony You?

Elizabeth I'm fine, too.

Tony   Good. You been standing there long?

Elizabeth   No.

Tony   You've changed, you look great. Not that you didn't always look great, you know. But you just look even more . . .

Elizabeth   Thank you. You look . . .

Tony   Old.

Elizabeth   Older maybe. It's been a while, hasn't it? Reggie and I were trying to remember . . .

Tony   Where is he?

Elizabeth   He'll be here soon.

Tony   I better go and leave you both to it.

Elizabeth   No, he's driving up separately. He was in LA when we heard the news. He couldn't fly back until today.

Tony   I know. So that was you I saw driving?

Elizabeth   Yes.

Tony   Impressive. How's he getting here?

Elizabeth   In his car.

Tony   His car?

Elizabeth   Yes, that's mine.

Tony   Oh, that's yours. Very nice.

Elizabeth   Yes. It was my birthday present.

Tony   Gosh. Happy birthday. So what's he driving then?

Elizabeth   Oh, you know men. An impractical old sports car. Since the kids have been older he's reverted back to his childhood.

Tony   Yes. What make is it?

Elizabeth   Um . . . Oh God, sorry, I've just thought, are you in here?

Tony   No. No. I was just . . . you know using the er . . .

Elizabeth   Which room are you in then?

Elizabeth *hangs her dress-hanger in the wardrobe.*

Tony   Next door, in my old room.

Elizabeth   Really? That's OK, is it?

Tony   Yes it's OK. Look, I'd better let you get ready. I'll see you later.

Elizabeth   It's a sad day, Tony.

Tony   Yes . . . I was very sorry to hear about your mum.

Elizabeth   You didn't come to the funeral.

Tony   No. Sorry. I was going to, but we had Claire visiting last Christmas and it would have been a bit difficult.

Elizabeth   Has she come with you today?

Sheila *enters.*

Tony *and* **Sheila**   No –

Sheila   – she hasn't. Hello, Elizabeth. How are you?

Elizabeth   Sheila.

They embrace and kiss.

Sheila   Look at her, Tony. Didn't I say how she'd look?

Tony   You did.

Sheila   As beautiful as ever.

Elizabeth   You too. I love the dress.

Sheila   Thank you. Tony thinks it's too tarty, don't you, dear?

Tony   I didn't say that.

Elizabeth   It's lovely. But if I were you, I wouldn't lean forward.

Sheila Yes. There should only be one stiff at a funeral. (*She laughs.*)

Tony Drink, anyone?

Sheila Oh, lucky you, being put in here. Such a lovely room. This is beautiful.

She refers to the necklace **Elizabeth** *is wearing.*

Elizabeth Thank you. I've just actually had it made.

Sheila Look at this, Tony. Wonderful. It's so intricate.

Elizabeth It was based on my wedding ring.

Sheila Was it? Where is your wedding ring?

Elizabeth Um.

Sheila Oh dear. Where's Reggie?

Tony Arriving separately.

Sheila Oh no. Nothing's wrong between you two, is it?

Elizabeth No Sheila, nothing.

Sheila Oh good. I'd hate the thought of that. There'd be no ravens in the Tower when that happened. It's bad luck not to wear your ring, you know.

Elizabeth I'm having it altered.

Sheila Are these diamonds real?

Elizabeth Well, they're diamonds.

Sheila Did Reggie get it for you? Tony never buys me anything like this.

Elizabeth No, it's one of mine.

Sheila Funny, isn't it, you and Tony ending up in the same business. He makes them you sell them.

Tony Cut them.

Elizabeth Design them.

Sheila   Exactly, he cuts them up and you stick them back together. I've been telling him for years, why doesn't he just slip a few into his pocket, no one would ever know, they're so small. I mean, I didn't marry a nice Jewish boy just so I could taste his mother's gefilte fish. But he's too much of a coward. I told him if he ever got caught, Reggie'd get him off. How are the twins?

Elizabeth   Good. Very good. They'll be at the church.

Sheila   Great. Isn't that great? Tony, the twins are going to be at the church.

Tony   It'll be nice to see them again.

Sheila   I bet they've grown.

Elizabeth   Since they were eight, yes, I imagine they have. They'll both be a bit nervous today, they're waiting on their A-level results.

Tony   That makes me feel old.

Elizabeth   Your Claire must be older.

Sheila   Yes, but she's not doing A-levels.

Elizabeth   No. Stephen's getting to look more like Reggie every day. I don't know who Samantha takes after.

Sheila   It's lucky they weren't identical then for her sake.

Elizabeth   You can't have mixed-sex identical twins.

Sheila   Can't you?

Elizabeth   No.

Tony   This old sports car he drives. It wouldn't be a Ferrari by any chance, would it? A red Ferrari Dino 246 GTB. The most beautiful sports car ever made.

Elizabeth   You sound like Reggie.

Tony   Jesus Christ! Slow down, man! This is the country, not a race track. He's just entering the chicane. I'm going to go and get ready.

Tony *exits.*

Sheila   He's a bit nervous. He's been so looking forward to seeing him again.

Elizabeth   Has he? Yes. Same with Reggie.

Sheila   They haven't seen each other since their mum died.

Elizabeth   I know. Look, if you don't mind, it's been a long drive, I'd like to . . .

Elizabeth *exits into the bathroom.*

Sheila   I'll leave you to it, then.

Sheila *exits.*

Scene Nine

The past.

Louis *enters from the bathroom. He is dressed in an expensive suit. He brushes his hair in the mirror. There is a knock on the door.*

Louis   Come in.

The door opens slightly.

Bella (*offstage*)   Do you mind if I use the mirror? Mine's too short.

Louis   Oh. Um. No. Come in.

Bella *enters wearing a wedding dress. She looks stunning.* **Louis** *stares at her, lost for words.*

Bella   You look nice.

Louis   Thank you. You look . . .

Bella   Thank you.

Louis   Should I go?

Bella   No, that's fine. If it's fine with you.

Louis   Yes, it's fine with me . . . I bought you some flowers. I've put them in the hall.

Bella   Yes, I saw them. My favourites, you know.

Louis   Are they? Good.

Bella   Are we doing the right thing, Louis?

Louis   Yes.

Bella   I love you.

Bobbie *enters, dressed in her best outfit.*

Bobbie   Oh, there you are. Everyone's looking for you. Arrr. Don't you look beautiful. Doesn't she look beautiful, Louis?

Louis   She does. She looks very beautiful.

Bobbie   Tom's going to be the happiest man in the world. Isn't he, Louis?

Louis   He is.

Bobbie   Your mother's just arrived.

Bella   Oh no.

Bobbie   She's bossing everyone around.

Bella   She does that.

Bobbie   She wants to see you, Louis.

Louis   Does she?

Bobbie   Yes . . . Now.

Louis   Oh. Right.

Bobbie   And find out where Tony is, I haven't seen him for ages.

Louis *exits.*

Bobbie How are you feeling?

Bella A little nervous.

Bobbie On my wedding day I wet myself.

Bella You didn't?

Bobbie I did. I was so nervous I peed my pants. The thing I was most scared about was that the two families wouldn't get on.

Bella And did they?

Bobbie No. Never did and never have. Louis' were so posh compared to mine. I was terrified that my dad was going to get drunk and start hitting people.

Bella Really?

Bobbie He liked a good fight. That was one of the reasons Louis married me, I think, fear . . . Don't worry, you're not even beginning to show.

Bella What?

Bobbie Am I right?

Bella Oh Bobbie, I'm so sorry. I was going to tell you. How did you know? . . . I wanted to say but I didn't know how. I couldn't . . . you know, because of . . .

Bobbie Don't be silly. These things happen. She's in heaven now. She's in heaven now. I know she is. She's in heaven, I know . . . Come on now, let's not be sad, this is a happy day. Even happier now. Everyone must be happy.

Bella Yes.

Bobbie How did Tom react?

Bella Um, well.

Bobbie You have told him!?

Bella Of course. He's delighted, if not a little shocked.

Bobbie Men always need a bit of a push. Didn't I say so?

Bella I'm doing the right thing then, yes?

Bobbie Yes, Bella, I'm sure you are.

Bella But Dad always pictured me under the chuppah.

Bobbie Tom's a very good man.

Bella He is. Yes. He is.

Bella *starts to cry.* **Bobbie** *comforts her.*

Bobbie Don't worry, everything will be all right.

Louis *enters.*

Louis You mother said we should be heading off.

Bella Well then, we must.

Louis Apparently it's bad luck to have lilies, so she's thrown them out.

Bobbie Who brought lilies?

Louis I did.

Bobbie Well, she's right.

Louis Tony says he doesn't want to go. He's refusing to come out of his room.

Bobbie Oh, not again. I'll see to him.

Louis Well then, shall we?

Louis *extends his arm for* **Bella** *to take.* **Bobbie** *arranges her dress.* **Louis** *escorts her out of the room.* **Bobbie** *watches the two as they exit, she then looks at herself in the mirror.*

Bobbie Louis! Louis!

Louis *returns.*

Louis What?

Bobbie I want to have another baby.

Bobbie *walks out.* **Louis** *follows her.*

Scene Ten

The present.

Elizabeth *appears from the bathroom in a long white towelling dressing gown.* **Reggie** *enters from the landing. He is tall, handsome, with a full head of hair, and is wearing a perfectly tailored black suit. They stare at each other, then very gradually come towards each other and start to kiss.*

Elizabeth   Reggie. Wait. I've the present I know you've always wanted.

She opens her robe to him. He stares at her lower body.

Reggie   Oh my God, you did it.

Elizabeth   I did it for you. Don't you like it?

Reggie   I love it. It's looks beautiful there.

Elizabeth   I've had a necklace made to match.

Reggie   Does it hurt?

Elizabeth   Only if it gets caught.

Reggie   You look so . . .

Reggie *breaks down in tears.*

Elizabeth   Oh, sorry. I'm so sorry. I thought you'd . . . I'm so sorry. There, it's OK. I'm sorry. I thought it might help. What was I thinking?

Reggie   Sorry. But seeing you stand there. Alive. It's just you and me now.

Elizabeth   And the kids.

Reggie   We've taken over. We're next.

Elizabeth   Oh sweetheart. Let me get you a drink. I tried to ring you on Wednesday night but the man at the hotel said you hadn't been back.

Reggie   Yes, the meeting went on quite late. Why has
Nina put us in here?

Elizabeth   Don't worry, he hadn't slept in here all this
year.

Reggie   So where was he when . . . when he died?

Elizabeth   Next door, in Tony's old room. You're late.
Was the flight delayed?

Reggie   No. I stopped off at the funeral parlour. I wanted
to see him one more time.

Elizabeth   Oh. What . . . what was it like?

Reggie   What's happened to this village? Every time I come
back I'm shocked as to how much it's changed. Jake's Funeral
Emporium isn't just Jake's Funeral Emporium any more.
He's had to diversify. His words not mine. It's now Jake's
Cakes.

Elizabeth   Jake's Cakes?

Reggie   Well, he's had the decency to rename the funeral
parlour but he still owns both of them. He provides coffee
out front and coffins out back. Apparently not enough
people are dying any more, but everyone needs cake. And
from what I could see he was right. Rushed off his feet he
was, so his son showed me through. Obsequious little shit.
'Would sir like me to leave you whilst you visit?' Visit!?
Visit!? I said, 'Sir would, yes,' so he scurried off to put some
froth on a cappuccino. (*Referring to his whisky.*) I could have
done with this then. (*As he tastes it.*) Uggh.

Elizabeth   Carry on. Tell me. I want to know. I always
thought I should have gone and seen Mum, but I was too
scared.

Reggie   I really wasn't prepared. It wasn't him.

Elizabeth   Who was it?

Reggie   No, it was him, but . . . Not the man I knew. And they'd dressed him in a blue suit. Dad wouldn't have been seen dead in a blue suit. Oh God. And they'd brushed his hair into a side-parting and put make-up on him. On Dad! He looked like Bob Hope.

Elizabeth   Oh God.

Reggie   I wish I hadn't gone. And do you know another thing, my tightfisted brother has had him put in their economy casket. Economy casket? I'm surprised he didn't go one better and buy it as a flat-pack from Ikea.

Elizabeth   Oh, sweetheart.

Reggie   I assume that's his Rover in the drive.

Elizabeth   Yes.

Reggie   Have you seen him?

Elizabeth   Briefly.

Reggie   Have they brought Claire?

Elizabeth *shakes her head.*

Reggie   What an ignominious end.

Elizabeth   Come here.

Reggie   I loved that man.

Elizabeth   I know you did.

Reggie   I did.

They hug.

Elizabeth   I know. Would you like me to get dressed?

Reggie *nods.*

Elizabeth   Perhaps you're right. I don't want to spend the whole day oozing . . . I'll have a quick shower, because I am rather sweaty from travelling.

Reggie Mmm.

Elizabeth I feel really . . . dirty.

Reggie Oh God. You're so right, come here.

They kiss passionately.

Elizabeth I love you.

Reggie I love you too.

Reggie's *mobile phone rings.*

Elizabeth Bugger!

Reggie Shit! . . . It's Stephen.

Elizabeth Stephen! Their results! Answer it.

Reggie Hello, Stephen. Hello? Hello? Hold on, I can hardly hear you. Is that better? Good . . . Yes . . . Well?

Elizabeth How did he do?

Reggie Stop playing games, son.

Elizabeth How did he do?

Reggie Of course you've passed, we knew that, but what were your grades? . . . Two B's and a what? . . . a C!

Elizabeth Two B's and a C! Fantastic. Two B's and a C!

Reggie What was the C in?

Elizabeth What about Samantha?

Reggie I thought you were good at Spanish.

Elizabeth What about Samantha?

Reggie You were top last year.

Elizabeth Reggie!

Reggie And that was the most important one.

Elizabeth What about Samantha?

Reggie What about Samantha? . . . What? . . . All A's.
Wow. Fantastic. Huh. Beaten by your sister . . . What? . . .
Oh, OK . . . Bye. Don't be late . . . Bad signal. How about
that?

Elizabeth Mmm.

Reggie Straight A's.

Elizabeth Yes.

Reggie Now where were we?

Elizabeth We were getting ready for your Dad's funeral.

Reggie Yes. Yes?

Elizabeth We'll have to be quick.

Reggie Yes.

*They go into the bathroom: there is no mistaking what they are about to
do. There is a knock on the bedroom door.* **Reggie** *and* **Elizabeth**
immediately fall silent. There is another knock on the door.

Reggie (*offstage*) Leave it. Don't answer it.

Elizabeth (*offstage*) We can't. You go, I'm not dressed.

Reggie What, like this?

There is another knock on the door.

Scene Eleven

The past.

Bobbie *comes out of the bathroom in a nightdress and gets onto the
bed.*

Bobbie Who is it?

Bella (*offstage*) It's me.

Bobbie Come in, sweetie.

Bella *enters.*

Bobbie   Oh Bella, I do so miss you these days.

Bella   Louis said you wanted to see me. He said you weren't well.

Bobbie   Oh, not really. You know, just the usual, I'm afraid.

Bella   Oh dear.

Bobbie   Yes. Oh well. They said it might be more difficult now.

Bella   What? Who?

Bobbie   The doctors. You know, after . . .

Bella   Oh.

Bobbie   There's always next month. Where is he, then? You did bring him?

Bella   Yes. He's just outside. I was going to take him through into Tony's room. He wants to play with him.

Bobbie   He's not a toy. Bring him here, I want to see him.

Bella   Are you sure?

Bobbie   Yes. Stop it. Yes.

Bella   All right.

Bella *gets the carry-cot from outside the door.*

Bobbie   Pop him down here. Isn't he beautiful? Ooo, I could almost eat him. Look, he's opened his eyes. Hello. Hello. Davie, Davie, Davie.

Bella   It's David.

Bobbie   Yes. David. There's a good boy. Oh, a smile for Aunty Bobbie.

Bella   It'll be wind.

Bobbie   It's not wind. You ignore her. Horrid Mummy.

Bella   Yes . . . Mummies are horrid, aren't they?

Bobbie   Don't be silly.

Bella   Mine is.

Bobbie   Oh no, what's she done now?

Bella   I can't turn round and she's not there. I put a cup down and she's washed it up. I get up from the sofa and she plumps the cushions. She's reorganised all my cupboards. She does everything, the washing, the dusting, the vacuuming, she's even painted the baby's bedroom.

Bobbie   You poor thing.

Bella   It's driving me demented. And she has an opinion on everything. How I should run my life. How I should really be breast-feeding. When he should be put to bed. When to pick him up. When not to pick him up. I mean, whose baby is he?

Bobbie   Louis wouldn't let my mother in the house.

Bella   Well, good for Louis.

Bobbie   Hardly ever saw her again after we got married. What does Tom say?

Bella   Say? Instruct more like. He's never there. He's always off somewhere, doing his stupid manoeuvres. And he's as bad as her, he talks to me like I'm one of his corporals. He's insisting now that David's christened. So on top of all this I'm in the middle of a religious war. What with him playing Commander-in-Chief and her crying at me all day that my father would be turning in his grave at the very thought of it, I don't know how I'm supposed to cope, I really don't. I'm going to tell her to pack her bags and go . . . Only I can't, of course.

Bobbie   Why not?

Bella   How would I finish my studies?

Bobbie   Why don't you leave him with me?

Bella   . . . No.

Bobbie   I'll look after him and you can spend more time helping Louis in the office.

Bella   No, I couldn't.

Bobbie   Which would then mean Louis could spend more time at home.

Bella   Oh. Yes.

Bobbie   He doesn't even want to touch me these days.

Bella   Doesn't he?

Bobbie   There was a time I wasn't safe to walk around this house without a bodyguard. He saw me as some moving target. It was like we were playing one of those commando game thingummies your Tom's always going on. He'd leap on me anywhere, anytime, and there was no stopping him once he got going. When he wanted it he got it. I'd have to creep about checking behind doors. Once he hid in that wardrobe – gave me such a scare I almost had a heart attack. I put my hand in to get a dress and before I knew it I was on my back, half my clothes were off, his trousers were round his ankles. I tried to stop him, I was trying to tell him.

Bella   What?

Bobbie   That I wasn't on my own. I'd come back for lunch with Mrs Partridge. You should have seen the look on her face. But now it's like getting blood out of a stone. He's not doing his duty.

Bella   What? Not at all?

Bobbie   Oh no, not . . . not at all.

Bella   Oh. Good.

Bobbie   What's your Tom like in bed?

Bella   Bobbie!

Bobbie   Don't be so pre-war. I won't tell anyone. Is he clean?

Bella   What do you mean?

Bobbie   You know, in his ways.

Bella   Yes . . . Very.

Bobbie   Good. Men should be clean. So what's he like?

Bella   Nice.

Bobbie   That doesn't sound very good.

Bella   Thoughtful.

Bobbie   Ooo dear.

Bella   Maybe a bit . . .

Bobbie   What? A bit what?

Bella   Military.

Bobbie   Military? Why? Does he wear his uniform?

Bella   No.

Bobbie   Does he stand by the bed and salute?

Bella   No. You know. Precise and regular.

Bobbie   What does that mean?

Bella   It means he rises at the same time each morning.

The women collapse in a fit of giggles.

Bella   I'd better be going. Louis's waiting for this case study. Oh dear, I think this little one could do with a feed.

Bobbie   I could do it.

Bella   No, I couldn't, I'd be putting you out.

Bobbie   You'd be doing me a favour.

Bella   Would I?

Bobbie   Yes.

Bella   Well, if you put it like that.

Bobbie   Good, that's sorted, then. We're going to have such fun, aren't we, Davie?

Bobbie *gets off the bed and takes the carry-cot towards the door.*

Bella   David.

Bobbie   David. Yes . . . Bella.

Bella   Yes.

Bobbie   Thank you . . . Tony! Tony! Guess who's come to visit.

Bobbie *exits.* **Bella** *takes a moment to contemplate their mutual pact.* **Bella** *exits.*

Scene Twelve

The present.

Elizabeth (*offstage*)   We'll finish this later.

Reggie (*offstage*)   Oh.

There is a knock on the door. **Sheila** *pokes her head in.*

Sheila   Hello. Hello. Hello. How are you doing?

Elizabeth *comes out of the bathroom. She has managed to put on her skirt and is in the process of putting on her blouse.*

Sheila   Oh, Sorry.

Elizabeth   No, it's fine. We're nearly ready. Reggie's just . . .

Sheila   No, we'll come back . . . Tony?

She had assumed **Tony** *was behind her, but no one enters.*

Elizabeth   No. Stay. We're almost there.

Reggie (*offstage, orgasm*) Arrgh.

Elizabeth   Reggie! Sheila's here.

Sheila   So how have you been?

Elizabeth   Since a few minutes ago or in the last ten years?

Sheila   In the last ten years.

Elizabeth   I've been fine. You?

Sheila   Oh yes. Fine.

Elizabeth   Good . . . It's bucketing down. What an awful summer we're having.

Sheila   It's because of global warming.

Elizabeth   I'm glad I packed our wellies.

Sheila   Oh. Is it going to be outside?

Elizabeth   What?

Sheila   The funeral.

Elizabeth   It's a burial.

Sheila   I know. But do we have to go outside?

Elizabeth   Only if you want to be there.

Sheila   Right . . .

Sheila *puts her hand to her mouth.*

Elizabeth   Were you going to say something?

Sheila   No. Just indigestion.

Elizabeth   I mean at the funeral.

Sheila   Me? No. You?

Elizabeth   Maybe . . . Reggie!

Sheila   Men. Never around when you need them. And always around when you don't. Was your mum buried?

Elizabeth   Cremated . . . Reggie!

Sheila   That's neater. I don't like the thought of the world cluttered up with rotting bodies. Tell me, did she actually die on Christmas Day itself?

Elizabeth   Yes.

Sheila   Huh . . . All that preparation . . . When's the will being read?

Elizabeth   What?

Sheila   I was just wondering.

Elizabeth   I don't know. Apparently no one can find it.

Sheila   Where is it?

Elizabeth   Well if we knew that . . .

Sheila   Does that mean we can all pick what we want?

Elizabeth   Reggie!!

Sheila   It's just that I know Tony's always loved that clock in the hall and I thought what with him being . . . the eldest.

Reggie *comes out of the bathroom.*

Reggie   Hello, Sheila. Hello. How are you? As beautiful as ever, I see.

Sheila   Reggie. Wow. Look at you. Ooo, in the words of your dear old mum, I could almost eat you. Tony! Your gorgeous brother's here.

Reggie   Let's all have a drink.

Elizabeth   Yes.

Sheila   Why not? It's so nice, it's not often we're all together, is −?

Reggie   No.

Sheila   Oh Reggie – I'm sorry. I'm being insensitive.

Reggie   No, no.

Sheila   I'm forgetting. It's such a sad day. Could I have a spot of water with mine, Reggie?

Reggie *goes into the bathroom.*

Sheila   Me and my big mouth.

Tony *enters, wearing the brightly coloured tie* **Sheila** *gave him.*

Sheila   Oh there you are. You're wearing it. Looks lovely. It's his birthday.

Elizabeth   Happy birthday.

Tony   Thank you.

Sheila   Tony doesn't have much luck with birthdays. Bit like you and Christmas.

Elizabeth   Reggie, Tony's here.

Reggie *comes out of the bathroom.*

Reggie   Tony. Good to see you. Good to see you.

Tony   You too.

Reggie   Yes. Good to see you.

Tony   Yes.

Sheila   All four of us together again.

Reggie   Yes.

Tony   Yes.

Elizabeth   Yes.

Sheila   It's been a while.

Elizabeth   It has, hasn't it?

Sheila   Yes.

Reggie   Since Mum died.

Tony Yes.

Elizabeth Yes.

Reggie Drink, Tony? Drink?

Tony Sorry?

Reggie Would you like a drink?

Tony Yes. Yes please.

Reggie Good. Good.

Sheila I was a bit worried, Reggie, that something terrible must have happened.

Reggie Why's that, Sheila?

Sheila Elizabeth's not wearing her ring.

Reggie Don't worry, it's in a safe place.

Sheila We wouldn't know what to do if you two split up. Would we, Tony?

Tony No.

Elizabeth Make mine a large one, Reggie.

Reggie Here we are. It's only a blend, I'm afraid. I don't know where it came from.

He hands a drink to **Tony**. **Sheila** *offers* **Elizabeth** *a cigarette.*

Sheila Ciggy?

Reggie I'm afraid we've both just given up.

Sheila Oh, go on. Special occasion.

Elizabeth Sod it, Reggie, I'm having one.

Sheila Reggie?

Reggie Oh, all right then.

Sheila Look at that tan. I bet you didn't get that in Bognor.

Reggie I was surprised, Tony, you didn't arrange all this for a synagogue.

Sheila   Yes, why didn't we?

Tony   This isn't Golder's Green.

Elizabeth   I'm sure Tony would have, Reggie, if there'd been one locally.

Tony   And we couldn't have had it on a Saturday, could we?

Reggie/Sheila   Well, no, obviously but . . . / I didn't think you wanted . . .

Tony   Anyway, he wasn't fussed about all that stuff, I know I'm not, and I'm sure as hell you're not.

Silence.

Sheila   Good health, everyone.

Tony/Reggie   Cheers/L'chayim.

The clock in the hall chimes.

Sheila   Listen to that, it's so beautiful. Do you like clocks, Reggie?

Reggie   Well . . . not especially.

Sheila   Right.

Tony   The hearse is late.

Reggie   Is it? Oh.

Tony   Yes. I hope they hurry up, we mustn't miss our slot.

Reggie   Sorry?

Tony   We have an allocated time-slot.

Reggie   What do you mean?

Tony   There's a wedding at four and it's not a good idea to clash, it scares the newlyweds.

Reggie   But that doesn't . . . at four?

Sheila   Whose car should we go in?

Reggie   Aren't we all going in the funeral car . . . There is a funeral car, isn't there?

Tony   They had one, but it's actually being used for the wedding.

Reggie   Oh.

Tony   Well, it's just a black shiny car. They stick a white ribbon on or take it off.

Reggie   They do weddings too?

Tony   Apparently not enough people are –

Reggie   – dying any more. Yes, I heard.

Tony   I had thought we would probably walk.

Sheila/Elizabeth   Walk!?

Tony   Well it's only up the road. Obviously it's too wet now but . . . anyway it seemed pointless, we've all got transport.

Reggie   Right.

Tony   And Jake was a bit short on pall-bearers so I volunteered you and me to help out.

Reggie   But he does make exceedingly good cakes.

Elizabeth   Reggie.

Sheila   I want to go in the Ferrari. Take me in the Ferrari, Reggie.

Tony   No. We'll all go in mine.

Sheila   I'm not letting you behind a wheel with the amount you've stashed away. Open this for me would you, Reggie?

Sheila *hands* **Reggie** *a hand-cream jar she has been struggling with.*

Tony   Everyone drinks and drives in the country, it's expected. Pubs would go out of business if they didn't.

Reggie *opens the jar.*

Sheila Do you work-out?

Reggie Sometimes.

Sheila I'm surprised you ever let this one out your sight.

Reggie I've read very good reports about that Rover.

Tony Have you? Yes, it won an award.

Reggie Did it? What for?

Tony Reliability.

Reggie Great.

Tony Yours is nice.

Reggie Thank you.

Tony Reliable?

Reggie I don't use it that often.

Tony Bet it's a bit pricey on petrol.

Reggie Probably.

Tony You don't get much headroom in those either, do you?

Reggie No.

Tony What year is it?

Elizabeth We'll take mine. That seems to the best solution.

The phone rings. She snatches it up.

Elizabeth Yes? What? Who? It's OK, Nina I've got it. Say again . . . Jake? . . . Yes he's here.

Tony *assumes it is for him, but* **Elizabeth** *hands the phone to* **Reggie**.

Elizabeth Reggie.

Reggie   Reginald Ellis. Thank you, Nina, I have it. No, put the phone down, I'll handle it. Sorry, who's speaking? . . . Are we not expecting you? . . . I see . . . Where are you? (*To the room.*) They've broken down . . . I see. Why, may I ask, are you up there? (*To the room.*) They're up at Pitcher's Point . . . I see. (*To the room.*) The Old Ford Road's flooded. No, stay exactly where you are, we'll be with you in five minutes. (*He puts the phone down.*) The hearse has broken down. Do you have a mobile?

Tony *shakes his head.*

Reggie   OK, we'll go together. Sheila, go with Elizabeth, take Nina, and warn the vicar we'll be late, but we'll be there.

Elizabeth   OK, Reggie, come on Sheila.

Elizabeth *exits.*

Tony   Didn't he want to speak to me?

Reggie   No.

Tony   Right. I'll get my coat.

Tony *exits.*

Sheila   Why can't I go in the Ferrari?

Reggie   We're not going in the Ferrari. We're going to take your hatchback.

Sheila   Why do you need to take the hatchback?

Reggie   Because if the hearse won't start . . .

Sheila   Oh no.

Reggie *exits.*

Sheila   I've just cleaned it out. I was going to put the clock in there.

Sheila *exits.*

Act Two

Scene One

The present.

Sheila *and* **Elizabeth** *enter. They are wet and dishevelled.* **Elizabeth** *has one of her heels broken.* **Elizabeth** *goes into the bathroom to fetch a towel for* **Sheila**. **Sheila** *pours them both a drink.* **Elizabeth** *comes out of the bathroom and gives* **Sheila** *the towel, then changes her shoes.* **Sheila** *hands her a drink, they both sit on the bed and silently contemplate.*

Reggie (*offstage*)   They should have checked it this morning then.

Tony (*offstage*)   Saturday's a busy day for them.

Reggie (*offstage*)   What the hell's that supposed to mean?

Reggie *and* **Tony** *enter. They are soaked and very muddy.*

Tony   We didn't have any choice.

Reggie   You didn't give us any.

Tony   And what would you have done? Sent everyone home?

Reggie   If needs be.

Tony   Needs be? Needs be? Needs did be. What, come back another day just because there's a little bit of water in the grave?

Sheila   Urggh. Makes me shudder.

Tony   Hang on now, you agreed with me.

Sheila   I know I did, but it was horrible. It's like we were drowning him.

Reggie   They should have checked it.

Tony   These things happen overnight. It's something to do with underground streams. I don't know.

Sheila   It'd be like going to bed with wet clothes on.

Elizabeth   Sheila, please.

Tony   The coffin would have been watertight.

Reggie   Not the one you bought wouldn't have.

Elizabeth   Come on now, let's all go and get changed. Everybody's downstairs waiting for us.

Tony   I'm not going down, I can't face Nina.

Elizabeth   Everything's going to be fine.

Reggie   We should have delayed it until they'd pumped it out.

Tony   What, with that wedding party already arriving? It was do it then or send everyone home and that would have been worse.

Sheila   That poor bride. I felt for her.

Reggie   Maybe if your mate Jake had filled up with petrol –

Tony   They broke down.

Reggie   So they say.

Sheila   Such a pretty girl.

Reggie   What an undignified way to arrive. Hanging out of the back of your car, covered in a bin-liner.

Tony   That was your idea.

Reggie   If I'd known we were about to plunge him into a foot and a half of stagnant water –

Sheila   Oh gosh.

Reggie   – I wouldn't have bothered.

Elizabeth   Look, well, what's done is done.

Reggie   And I've never seen a funeral service conducted at such terrifying speed. I thought the vicar was auditioning for *Just a Minute*. Though I'd have buzzed him on deviation. Did he actually know Dad?

Elizabeth   He did say some nice things, Reggie.

Reggie   And he had the cheek to check his watch while I was speaking.

Tony   We all did. I never got a chance to say anything.

Reggie   Did you want to?

Elizabeth   I want to get changed, please.

Tony   So are you going to criticise all my arrangements?

Elizabeth   Reggie! Come on, let's all go and get changed. Let's not say anything we . . .

Reggie   You employed an incompetent firm of funeral directors whose main speciality is cakes and you practically had him buried in a pine box.

Tony   A simple funeral. A simple coffin. It's the Jewish way.

Reggie   Jewish? You said . . .

Tony   You wouldn't understand.

Reggie   What!?

Elizabeth   No, Tony. Come on now, both of . . .

Reggie   You had the service at a church on the sabbath, hardly what I call a traditional Jewish funeral. You're about as Jewish as a . . . You had him embalmed, for Christ's sake.

Tony   Otherwise he wouldn't have kept til you got back.

Reggie   He's not a piece of meat. Tell me, did you go and see him?

Tony   No.

Reggie   I did and I wish I hadn't, the way they'd messed around with him. I wish I could remember him how he was.

Tony   I'd rather remember him how he is.

Reggie   That's my father you're talking about.

Tony   Only . . .

The painting of **Louis** *falls off the wall.*

Sheila/Tony/Reggie/Elizabeth   Oh Jesus Christ!/Shit!/
Arggh!/(*Screams.*)

They all jump and take a moment to collect themselves. Behind the painting a safe has been exposed.

Tony *helps himself to more whisky. He never allows his glass to be empty from now on.*

Sheila   It's a sign. He's speaking to us from the other side. I know about these things.

Elizabeth   No Sheila. Please. We don't believe in all that stuff.

Sheila   We've desecrated his tomb.

Tony   Look, the nail's just come out. It could have broken at any time.

At some point during the scene **Tony** *puts the painting back up.*

Sheila   How long's he been up there?

Tony   I don't know. Since we were kids.

Sheila   And he chooses today to fall down after he's being up there quite happily for half a century.

Elizabeth   It's a coincidence.

Sheila   It's a sign.

Elizabeth   Stop it, Sheila. Stop it. Look, it's been a traumatic day for everyone. We've all said things we don't mean. So let's go and get changed and try and remember some happy times. I'm sure one day we'll look back on this and laugh. Tony, Sheila, come on now.

Sheila   What's that?

Elizabeth   What does it look like?

Sheila   It looks like a safe.

Elizabeth   Then I guess that's what it is.

Sheila Has anyone opened it? . . . Well, don't you think we should? I mean, that's where I'd keep a will if I was going to . . .

Elizabeth YOU CAN HAVE THE FUCKING CLOCK!

Sheila *walks out.*

Reggie Tony?

Tony She'll be all right.

Reggie Arr.

As **Tony** *doesn't move,* **Reggie** *goes after* **Sheila**.

Reggie Sheila. Sheila, come back.

Tony We've got nowhere to put that clock even if we had it. Look stupid in our hall. It's bigger than our hall. Do you think anyone would mind if I had this?

He refers to the painting of the woman.

Elizabeth I don't know. I know Reggie has always . . .

Tony Do you remember your seventeenth birthday?

Elizabeth Um . . .

Tony I do. Not mine, yours. Reggie and I fought over you.

Elizabeth Really?

Tony Well, arm-wrestled, that was our way then. Course I was a lot older and always won. But not that time. I was going to ask you out to the pictures, but I made the mistake of telling Reggie. He went bananas, told me I was too old and too ugly to stand a chance and he was going to take you instead. So we arm-wrestled to see who would.

Elizabeth Didn't I have any say in this?

Tony We'd never fought like we did that day. He was getting difficult to beat, but I still had the edge. And then something happened. I looked up at him struggling, red-faced, using every ounce of his strength, refusing to give in, and I realised I didn't want to beat him. I couldn't bring myself to do it, I gradually let myself weaken and he won. So he was the one who got to take you to see *Doctor Zhivago*. I've always wondered what would have happened if I'd chosen to win.

Elizabeth   I really ought to get changed.

Reggie *enters*. **Elizabeth** *walks into the bathroom.*

Reggie   Everyone's in tears down there.

Tony   Mmm.

Reggie   Nina's in hysterics.

Tony   Hmm.

Reggie   She's been through quite a bit with our family.

Sheila *enters, carrying a small cardboard box.*

Sheila   The undertaker's turned up. He wants to see someone.

Elizabeth *comes out of the bathroom.*

Reggie   He'll need to after I'm finished with him.

Sheila   He asked me to give you this, Tony, to say sorry.

She hands the cardboard box to **Tony**.

Reggie   Let's all go down and accept his apology.

Tony   I'm not going anywhere.

Reggie   Come on.

Tony   No. You can do what you like at funerals. It's one of the few times in life when you're allowed to.

Reggie   Come on, Elizabeth.

Elizabeth   I want to get changed.

Tony   It's a cake.

Reggie   How thoughtful.

Reggie *makes to leave.*

Elizabeth Reggie!

Reggie We can't leave the kids down there on their own.

Elizabeth Stay here.

Silence.

Sheila According to Nina the safe's not locked.

Elizabeth You're right, I haven't had a chance to congratulate them yet.

Sheila They passed, did they?

Elizabeth Yes.

Reggie Samantha got straight A's.

Sheila Clever girl.

Reggie Chemistry, Physics and Maths. She's quite exceptional. She wants to be a scientist.

Sheila Really? Do you know if she's done Einstein's theory?

Elizabeth These are A-levels Sheila.

Sheila Oh yeah, of course.

Reggie She's not going to need to rely on any man for her meal-ticket.

Elizabeth Thank you very much.

Reggie No, I didn't mean . . . That's different, we had kids. You know that, if we were . . . (*Referring to the cake.*) Why are there dents in it?

Tony Where?

Reggie There. Two square dents.

Tony I don't know.

Reggie Well I do. That's where the happy couple would go.

Tony What?

Reggie It's a wedding cake. He's just taken off the plastic figures.

Sheila That poor young couple. All of us stomping through their party.

Tony I spoke to them and they seemed fine.

Reggie If he thinks he can get away with it by giving us this lousy cake, he's got another think coming.

Elizabeth I heard one of the little bridesmaids say, I heard her say, 'Why are they carrying that box, Mummy?' And do you know what her mother said. She said it was to keep dandelions in and we were going to bury it in the ground and then they would grow. I don't know why she said that, do you?

Tony You'll believe anything as a kid.

Elizabeth I like the thought that we get planted and grow again. Whenever I see dandelions I'll think of Louis.

Elizabeth *starts to cry.* **Tony** *tops everyone's drinks up.*

Sheila Does anyone know any good jokes?

Tony I don't think this is the time for jokes.

Sheila You said you could do what you like at funerals.

Tony Only the bereaved.

Sheila And what am I? Chopped liver? I think we should cheer up and make it all better. We should do it for Pop, it's what he would have wanted.

Tony Is it?

Sheila Yes, he loved to laugh.

Tony News to me.

Sheila Yes. We must. Please. He was such fun. I loved Louis.

Elizabeth So did I. He had a wonderful sense of humour. Sheila's right. Sorry. Sorry, Sheila.

Sheila It's just I like that clock. Louis liked that clock. We both liked it.

Elizabeth Yes. Sorry.

Tony I don't know any jokes.

Sheila Oh yes you do. What about the one with the man who pretends he has no hands, you know, and you do all the actions, and then he says, 'I don't know but I'm not touching it.'

Tony That's the punch-line.

Sheila Yes.

Reggie What do you get when you cross a lawyer with *The Godfather*?

Sheila Oh good. I don't know, Reggie, what do you get when you cross a lawyer with *The Godfather*?

Reggie An offer you can't understand.

Sheila That's very good. That's very funny.

Tony What's the difference between a dead dog in the road and a dead lawyer in the road? . . . There are skid marks in front of the lawyer . . . dog. Got that wrong.

Elizabeth How many lesbians does it take to change a light bulb?

Sheila Sorry, Elizabeth, I'd rather you didn't tell any lesbian jokes if you don't mind. My sister's one, you see.

Elizabeth Is she? Oh.

Sheila Splash of water with mine, Tony.

Tony *goes into the bathroom with the bottle of whisky and* **Sheila**'s *glass.*

Reggie Um. I've another one. I don't know if I should tell it, but it's quite funny.

Sheila Yes. Tell it. Go on. Go on, Reggie.

Reggie   All right. All right.

Sheila   No, wait for Tony. Tony, hurry up. Reggie's got a good one.

Tony *comes out of the bathroom with the glass but no bottle.*

Reggie   Right. There's a priest, a Buddhist and a rabbi, and they're all discussing what each would like to be said at their funeral. The priest said that he would like someone to say, 'There is a man who followed the path of Jesus.' The Buddhist said that he would like someone to say, 'There is a man who strived for enlightenment.' The rabbi said that he would like someone to say, 'LOOK! He's moving!'

Reggie's *laughter turns into crying.*

Sheila   Oh, Reggie. That's it, you let it out. It's good to let it out. There, there. Oh, I know one.

Reggie   I'm sorry. I'm so sorry.

Sheila   How does it go now, oh yes. There's this . . .

Elizabeth   No I don't think we should . . .

She and **Sheila** *comfort* **Reggie**.

Elizabeth   No. Oh yes. Go on, Sheila. Tell your joke. I want to hear your joke. Tell it for Pop.

Sheila   This is a really great one. You'll love this. There's this dear old lady and she's really upset because her husband Albert has just passed away. She goes to the undertaker's to have one last look at her dearly departed husband, but the moment she sees him, she starts crying. One of the undertakers rushes up to give her some comfort. Through her tears she explains that she is upset because her dear Albert was wearing a black suit, and it was his dying wish to be buried in a blue suit.

Elizabeth   Sheila.

Sheila   The undertaker apologises and explains that traditionally, they always put the bodies in a black suit, but he'd see what he could arrange.

Elizabeth   Sheila.

Sheila   Ssh. Ssh. The next day she returns to the undertaker's to have one last moment with Albert before his funeral the following day. When the undertaker pulls back the curtain, she manages to smile through her tears as Albert is decked out beautifully in a smart blue suit. She says to the undertaker 'Wonderful, wonderful, but where did you get that beautiful blue suit?" The undertaker replied, 'Well, yesterday afternoon, after you left, a man about your husband's size was brought in and he was wearing a blue suit. His wife explained that she was very upset as he had always wanted to be buried in a black suit.' The old lady smiled at the undertaker. He continued, 'After that, it was simply a matter of swapping the heads.'

Reggie   Excuse me.

Reggie *picks up the cake and exits.*

Elizabeth   Reggie!

Sheila   What did I say? Reggie told one about funerals. Reggie! (*She exits.*) Reggie. Sorry. I didn't mean anything by it.

Tony   Congratulations about the results . . . you know, for Stephen and Samantha. You must be very proud.

Elizabeth   We are. Yes. Thank you . . . How's Claire?

Tony   Good, thanks. She'd normally be at football with me today. She loves that.

Elizabeth   How is she, though?

Tony   She's not ill.

Elizabeth   No, I know.

Tony   She's not going to get any better, if that's what you mean.

Elizabeth   No, I didn't.

Tony   And she's not stupid either. She's the only woman I know who understands the offside rule.

Elizabeth Yes.

Tony She's fantastic, that's what she is.

Elizabeth What is it with men and their daughters? I've only ever been to a football match once. Your dad got tickets for Reggie and Stephen to go with him and see West Ham play.

Tony When?

Elizabeth You don't support them, do you?

Tony No. Fulham. So how come you went?

Elizabeth Well, Reggie couldn't make it in the end, so I went instead. It was a good day out, your dad knew the chairman and we all sat in the directors' box. But the best thing was that afterwards they gave Stephen the match ball, it had been signed by all the players, you should have seen his face. Unfortunately it got lost when we moved house, he was so upset.

Sheila *enters.*

Sheila I think you'd better come, Reggie's just punched the funeral man.

Elizabeth Bugger.

Sheila I'm so sorry.

Elizabeth Bugger.

Sheila I shouldn't have told that joke.

Elizabeth *exits.*

Sheila Aren't you coming to help?

Tony It doesn't take two to beat up an undertaker.

Sheila How dare she get all shirty over that clock. When you consider all the stuff they've got.

Tony Where's the whisky?

Tony *looks for the bottle of whisky.*

Sheila   That necklace alone must be worth a small fortune. And where's her wedding ring? There's something wrong between those two, you mark my words.

Sheila *exits.*

Tony   Where's the bloody whisky? Think. I went over there. Poured that. Then I went here. Poured that. (*He mimes having the bottle in his hand and trying to remember.*) Der. Der. Der . . . (*He arrives at a mirror and looks at himself.*) What's the difference between a dead dog in the road and a dead lawyer in the road? . . . There are skid marks in front of the dog. What's the difference between a dead dog in the road and a dead lawyer in the road? . . . There are skid marks in front of the dog. (*He starts to laugh.*) Swapping the heads! (*Remembering where he left the whisky.*) Ah yes.

Tony *goes into the bathroom.* **Elizabeth** *enters, pursued by* **Reggie**.

Elizabeth   What is it with men? Tell me, because I just can't work it out.

Reggie   He had it coming.

Elizabeth   You either have to punch it or fuck it.

Sheila *enters.*

Elizabeth   Get out!

Sheila *exits.*

Elizabeth   You think I wanted to have this done? To mutilate myself. I'm a fifty-three-year-old woman who's had her clitoris pieced in a vain attempt to add some spice so you wouldn't feel the need to shag everything that comes in a size ten or under. It's a pity I wasn't able to stomach a self-pitying, self-indulgent, whinging sort of man because I'm sure your brother would at least have been faithful.

Tony *closes the bathroom door.*

Elizabeth   Oh God . . . Tony? . . . Tony?

Tony (*offstage*)   I didn't hear anything.

Elizabeth   Tony . . .

Tony (*offstage*)   Go away.

Elizabeth *storms over to the wardrobe and takes out the dress-hanger.*

Elizabeth   Arggh. Bugger. Come on. We're going to go downstairs now, be nice to everyone, have the will read, then we're leaving. I'm not staying in this house a moment longer than is necessary.

Elizabeth *exits.* **Reggie** *follows.*

Scene Two

The past.

Bobbie *enters from the bathroom carrying the carry-cot. She sings 'Be Bop a Lula' by Gene Vincent quietly to the baby, replacing the word 'she' for 'he'.* **Bella** *enters.*

Bobbie   Sssh.

Bella   How's he doing?

Bobbie   He's just gone off.

Bella   Oh, shame.

Bobbie   I've traipsed him all over the place today. We've had such a lovely time splashing about in the rain.

Louis *enters.*

Louis   What a filthy night.

Bobbie   Sssh.

Louis   What?

Bobbie   Sssh. I've only just got him to sleep.

Louis   I've booked the table for eight.

Bobbie   John and Betty can't come, there'll only be six of us.

Louis No. Eight o'clock, twillup.

Bobbie Oh, silly me. Look what I bought for him.

She picks up a shopping bag and hands it to **Louis**. *Before he can look inside* **Bella** *takes it from him and takes out an over fancy baby's outfit.*

Bella Not another thing, Bobbie, you really didn't need to . . . Oh. Oh. Thank you. Lovely. Lovely. It's quite elaborate.

Bobbie Of course it is. It's for tomorrow. For his big day.

Bella I already have a christening outfit.

Bobbie It can't be as pretty as this, surely. Look, it's adorable. Please, he'd look lovely in it.

Bella No, but . . .

Bobbie Please.

Bella Um.

Bobbie What do you think, Louis?

Louis Well . . . er . . .

Bobbie Oh go on, Bella.

Bella Well . . .

Bobbie Pleeease. Pleeease.

Bella *nods.*

Bobbie Thank you. Thank you. And this. We'd like him to have this.

Louis Bobbie?

Bobbie A christening bracelet. I know he's a boy, but they don't mind at that age, do they? I haven't had it inscribed yet, but there's a place for it to go. See.

Bella It's beautiful. Thank you. Thank you very much. Both of you.

Bella *goes to take the carry-cot.*

Bobbie   You're not taking him, are you? Nina said she'd baby-sit for the both of them.

Bella   I need to go home and change before we go out. Oh my goodness, I'm late. I'm meeting Tom at the station.

Bobbie   No point taking him all the way home just so you can bring him back. It's such an awful night, you'll only disturb him. He's only just got off.

Bella   But I haven't seen him all day.

Bobbie   Another hour or so won't make any difference. Leave him here.

Bella   But I want to . . .

Bobbie   No Bella, don't be silly. She's being silly, isn't she Louis? Isn't she?

Bobbie *comes across to* **Louis** *and puts her arms round him.* **Bella** *watches.*

Louis   It does makes sense . . . This is for a boy, is it?

Bobbie   Of course it's for a boy, the ribbons are blue.

Louis   Did Tony choose it?

Bobbie   Stop it, you old grump. You leave him alone, he's fine.

Louis   Mmm. John and Betty can't come, why?

Bobbie   Their baby-sitter's let them down.

Louis   What a horrible night.

Bobbie   I hope it clears up for tomorrow, it gets so muddy up at that church.

Bella *kisses the baby.*

Bella   Bye.

Bella *exits.*

Louis So now tonight we have Beryl and Charles and Tom – what a combination.

Bobbie Tom wants to explain to us our duties and responsibilities as godparents.

Louis Jewish godparents! Whatever next. She should never have married out of the faith.

Bobbie Please don't be rude to him tonight.

Louis Well, make sure I don't sit next to him, then. The man's a prig and a bigot.

Bobbie He's funny.

Louis He's not funny, he's opinionated, there's a difference.

The bathroom door closes.

Louis What's going . . .?

Bobbie Tony's in there.

Louis Why? Tony!?

Bobbie Leave him.

Louis What's he doing in our bathroom?

Bobbie Having a bath. He wanted to bath in there.

Louis What's wrong with the other one?

Bobbie Nothing. I don't know. He won't leave me alone at the moment. It's driving me mad. (*An explosion of feeling from seemingly nowhere.*) It's driving me mad!

Louis All right. All right. Calm down. Calm down.

Bobbie Talk to me, Louis. Please talk about it.

Louis No. We have to put it behind us.

Bobbie She was your baby too.

Louis It doesn't do to keep raking it all up.

Pause

Bobbie   I think you might need to have a word with Tony. A father-and-son word.

Louis   He's seven!

Bobbie   A boy at his school has been going round telling everyone that babies come after a mummy and a daddy have a fight. I think you should put him straight.

Louis   I will . . . not tonight, but I will.

Bobbie *exits.* **Louis** *immediately goes over to the baby.*

Louis   Hello. little one. Don't you ever listen to a single word he says. He's a prig and a bigot. Look at you. You come to me, I'll set you straight.

Bella *bursts in.*

Bella   Are you sleeping with her again?

Louis   What?

Bella   Are you sleeping with her?

Louis   Ssh. Not now.

Bella   Are you?

Louis   We share a bed.

Bella   Are you still sleeping with her?

Louis   She's my wife.

Bobbie *enters.*

Bobbie   Still here, Bella?

Bella   I've changed my mind. I'm taking him with me.

Bobbie   No Bella, don't be silly.

Bella   I want to take him.

Bobbie   Stop, you'll wake him. Look at the weather.

Bella Please.

Bobbie Bella, stop.

Bella Give him here.

Bobbie No.

Bella Bobbie, let go.

Bobbie Louis, give her the keys to the car. Then you can pick Tom up, go and get changed, and you'll be back before you know it. Louis –

Louis *hands* **Bella** *the keys.*

Bobbie I'll put him through next door so we don't disturb him later.

Bobbie *exits with the baby.*

Bella Are you?

Louis She'd suspect if I didn't.

Bella Bastard.

Louis If we hadn't lost the baby all this would have been different.

Bella You'd have walked out on two children then, would you?

Louis No.

Bella So how would it have been different?

Louis I don't know . . . I'll make it be all right. I promise. I'll make it better.

Pause

Bella How? (*She exits.*)

Louis (*quietly*) I love you.

Louis *exits.*

Scene Three

The present.

Sheila *enters from the landing and makes her way across to the safe, but before she has an opportunity to open it there is a sound of retching coming from the bathroom.*

Sheila   Tony? Is that you in there? Tony?

More retching sounds.

Are you all right?

Reggie *enters.*

Reggie   We need to get going. Where's Tony?

Sheila   He's in there.

More retching sounds.

Reggie   Oh God.

Sheila   Has everyone gone?

Reggie   Just a few dregs left.

Sheila   Shall I open this, then, and see . . .?

Tony *enters from the bathroom carrying an empty bottle of whisky.*

Sheila   Tony? Are you all right?

Tony   Fine. Fine. I'm fine.

Sheila   You don't look fine. Where are you going?

Tony   I need another drink, I've just got rid of the last lot.

Reggie   I think you've had enough.

Tony   Enough already.

Tony *runs back into the bathroom to be ill again.*

Reggie   Let's get this over with. Sheila, would you fetch Elizabeth?

Sheila   Be careful, he's not a happy drunk.

Sheila *exits.*

Reggie Tony?

Tony *storms out of the bathroom.*

Tony What have you got against me?

Reggie Me!?

Tony Yes, you.

Reggie Nothing.

Tony Well, you have a funny way of not showing it.

Reggie Great.

Tony That's it, true to form, walk away.

Reggie If you think I'm staying here to let you drunkenly insult me . . .

Tony Well, hang around, I'll be sober shortly.

Reggie I've always hated you when you get like this.

Tony At last you said it. You hate me.

Reggie No I didn't.

Tony You wouldn't have said it unless you were thinking it. You've got no reason to hate me, you were the one he loved the most.

Reggie Oh God. OK. So he loved me more than you. So what?

Tony What?

Reggie What should I have done about it, make him love me less.

Tony You're saying that he did?

Reggie Yes, I am.

Tony But what makes you think . . .?

Reggie And because of it, you should be grateful.

Tony   Why?

Reggie   Because I'm now suffering more than you are.

Tony   Hah! Come on.

Tony *gets into position to arm-wrestle.*

Reggie   What the hell are you doing?

Tony   Your half of the inheritance against mine.

Reggie   Don't be stupid.

Tony   Too steep for you. You never were a true Ellis.

Reggie   Right. You asked for it.

Reggie *takes the challenge.*

Tony   Not like that, like this.

He makes **Reggie** *change the type of grip.*

Tony   Ready?

Reggie   Ready.

Tony   Take the strain. Go.

They start. **Tony**'s *comment implies* **Reggie** *hasn't.*

Tony   In your own time.

Reggie   Very funny.

Elizabeth *and* **Sheila** *enter.*

Elizabeth   Reggie! What are you doing?

Reggie   He started it.

Reggie *and* **Tony** *struggle. Initially* **Tony** *gets the upper hand.*

Elizabeth   Pathetic.

Elizabeth *goes over to the safe and opens it.*

Sheila   Come on, Tony, he's younger than you.

Tony   I'm winning, woman.

Sheila   Well, don't have a seizure. He gets out of breath walking to the pub. That's why our dog's so fat.

Elizabeth *hands* **Sheila** *a pile of papers from the safe.* **Reggie** *starts to fight back.*

Sheila   Careful, Reggie, you mind the seam of that jacket.

Elizabeth   Sheila! Will you sort through those.

Sheila   What's all that?

Elizabeth   Bobbie's jewellery.

Sheila   Let's see.

Tony   Are those Dad's cufflinks?

Elizabeth   I thought Pop would have cleared these out years ago.

Sheila   He probably couldn't bear to part with them.

Elizabeth   I don't blame him, they're beautiful. (*She holds up a necklace.*) She wore this one to our wedding.

Sheila   Oh, that was a lovely day.

Elizabeth   Yes. She wore it with that green and black Chinese-style dress. You remember. On someone else it would have been gaudy, on her it was just perfect. She had such style. A real Jewish princess.

Sheila   Which was bizarre, as she wasn't actually Jewish.

Elizabeth   Wasn't she?

Sheila   No, she'd taken the faith.

Elizabeth   Why did she tell me not to, then?

Sheila   Were you going to convert?

Elizabeth   I did think about it.

Sheila   Mmm. Me too.

Elizabeth   She warned me that to be accepted as a Jew you had to be born a Jew.

Sheila   Mmm. Good Lord, Tony. Look what I've found.

Reggie *now has the upper hand.*

Reggie   Give in.

Elizabeth   Gosh. Sheila look at this.

Sheila   What? . . . Ah. How sweet. It's so tiny.

Elizabeth   It's a christening bracelet.

Sheila   So it is. How odd.

Tony *is now losing.*

Tony   I've got you just where I want you.

Sheila   Tony, I've found your birth certificate. Tony . . .

Tony   I'm busy.

Sheila   You can get yourself a passport now. He's been using this as an excuse for as long as I can remember.

Elizabeth *picks up some papers.*

Tony   You're not going to win. You think you are, but you're not.

There is a look exchanged between **Sheila** *and* **Elizabeth**.

Tony   I'm not going to let you . . . I'm not.

Reggie, *seeing* **Elizabeth** *and* **Sheila** *staring at him, looks at* **Tony** *struggling.* **Reggie** *starts to lose.* **Tony** *wins.*

Tony   Yes. Yes. I won. I won.

Elizabeth   Yes. Congratulations. Well done. Very good.

Tony   I used the finger-rolling technique. Have you heard of that?

Reggie   No.

Tony   Thought not. It's how you win from a losing position. Ha. Ha. Ha.

Reggie   Congratulations.

Sheila   Yes, well done.

Tony   I knew it.

Reggie   Yes. The best man won.

Elizabeth   I think I may have found it.

Tony   I always was stronger than you.

Reggie   You were.

Tony   And you can't say it's better to be older, can you?

Reggie   I certainly can't.

Elizabeth   Yes, Last Will and Testament. Louis Judah Ellis.

Tony   Yes. Yes. The best man won.

Elizabeth   Well, now you're both even can we get on, please.

Tony   What? . . . You let me win.

Reggie   What?

Tony   You let me win.

Reggie   I didn't.

Tony   I was practically beaten and you let me win, like I was a little child.

Reggie   I didn't.

Tony   You did.

Reggie   I didn't.

Sheila   Of course he didn't, did he, Elizabeth?

Elizabeth   No.

Tony   Did you let me win?

Reggie   No.

Tony   You did. You let me win.

Reggie   I didn't.

Tony   Admit it. You let me win.

Reggie   All right, I let you win.

Elizabeth   Reggie!

Tony   I knew it. I knew it. I was right.

Reggie   Yes, you were right.

Tony   I am sometimes, you know. I'm sometimes right.

Sheila   I know you are.

Tony   I am.

Elizabeth   Enough. Reggie, look, he'd only just written this.

Reggie   Really? When?

Elizabeth   Last December. New Year's Eve.

Reggie   God.

Sheila   What was he writing his will for on New Year's Eve?

Elizabeth   I don't know.

Sheila   I told you we should have come back for Christmas . . . No, I mean, he was obviously depressed and lonely.

Reggie   Yes, we should have come back.

Tony   Are you just saying that?

Sheila   Do you think he knew he was going to die?

Elizabeth   We're all going to die.

Sheila   No, but soon. Maybe he was ill or maybe he wanted to.

Reggie   What are you saying?

Sheila   Nothing.

Tony   Were you just saying that?

Reggie   Saying what?

Tony   That you let me win? Just because I beat you?

Reggie   Oh God.

Tony   Were you?

Reggie   Tell me what you want me to say and I'll say it.

Tony   I want to know the truth.

Sheila   Oh, Tony.

Tony   I want to know the truth.

Tony *sees the baby's christening bracelet and picks it up.*

Sheila   Who writes their will on New Year's Eve? It's a time for looking forward.

Reggie   What did he have to look forward to? Everyone dead he's ever known. Apart from dear old Nina, who was the only one who really looked after him. I wouldn't blame him if he'd left all his money to her. Is that everything?

Elizabeth   It's all that's there.

Sheila   He can't cut us out just because we didn't come back for Christmas.

Reggie   Come on, bring that stuff. Nina should be with us for this.

They all leave apart from **Tony,** *who is left holding the bracelet. He examines it and tries to read the inscription.*

Tony   There's no name on this. I chose this.

He picks up the painting and puts it back on the wall. He talks to his father.

I chose this.

Sheila *returns.*

Sheila   Tony?

Tony   There's no name on it.

Sheila   What? Come on.

Sheila *exits.* **Tony** *exits.*

Scene Four

The past.

Bobbie *enters from the bathroom. She is wearing her best outfit.* **Louis** *enters from the landing, wearing a suit but no tie. He is carrying the carry-cot with Davie in.*

Louis   David. David. David. What is to be done? Things have got a little . . .

Bobbie   What are you doing?

Louis   I was asked to put him down for a bit.

Bobbie   No, not yet, or he won't sleep later. I'll need to feed him first.

Louis   He looks tired.

Bobbie   We need to keep him awake.

Bobbie *picks up the carry-cot and makes to exit.*

Louis   Bobbie

Bobbie   Yes, Lou-lou.

Louis   Can we talk?

Bobbie   I have to go and see to the guests.

Louis   Bobbie, sit down please . . . Sit down.

Bobbie *sits on the bed.*

Bobbie   Yes, Lou-lou.

Louis   Where's Tony?

Bobbie   He's in the garden.

Louis Oh yes. I see him. He's growing up fast. Turning into quite a lad. Bobbie. I, er . . . The thing is . . . Um. We have a problem.

Bobbie I know we do. We have to decide what's for the best.

Louis Yes.

Bobbie We should adopt him.

Louis What?

Bobbie It's what Bella and Tom would want.

Louis They're dead for Christ's sake!

Bobbie It's what Bella would have wanted.

Louis She hardly wanted to die.

Bobbie I know she didn't.

Louis If it wasn't for . . . for us insisting she took the stupid car.

Bobbie I wish that too, Louis.

Louis Why did we?

Bobbie We couldn't have known. But we did and now we have to make it right. We must do the right thing.

Louis What about Bella's mother? Don't you think she'll have something to say about this?

Bobbie She won't want to look after a little baby at her age.

Louis This is ridiculous.

Bobbie If she agrees, then we'll adopt him. Bring him up as if he's our own. More than our own. He needs special love to help him through this.

Louis No, Bobbie.

Bobbie This is how it was meant to be.

Louis   What are you talking about?

Bobbie   God's given us his gift back.

Louis   No.

Bobbie   If it hadn't been for me he'd have died in the car with them.

Louis   Don't say that.

Bobbie   I saved his life, Lou-lou.

Louis   But we need to speak about . . .

Bobbie   There's nothing more to say.

Louis   But Bobbie . . .

Bobbie   Bella was my best friend and she'd want me to look after him.

Louis   Maybe, but . . .

Bobbie   We have to think of the child, do what's best for him.

Louis   No. No.

Bobbie   Losing the baby was the most terrible thing that has ever happened to me.

Louis   Please, Bobbie.

Bobbie   But do you know what the worst thing about it was? It was waiting in the hospital for you to come. (*There is an implied question here that is never answered.*) I never held her. They took her away, they said it was for the best. I wanted to take her in my arms and sing to her, make it better, make her be alive. Let me have him, Lou-Lou. Please.

Louis   She'll never agree.

Bobbie   I think she will.

Louis   We can't ask her that. Not now. Not ever.

Bobbie   Speak to her, Louis. I'm sure you can make her see sense . . . He needs feeding. Come on, Reggie.

Louis Bobbie.

Bobbie Davie. Come on, Davie. (*She takes the carry-cot and exits.*)

Louis Oh God. What have I done? Help me, Bella. I miss you.

Louis *goes into the bathroom.*

Scene Five

The present.

Reggie *enters from the landing, hotly pursued by* **Tony**.

Tony I'm not accepting this.

Reggie Why not?

Tony Because it's not fair.

Elizabeth (*offstage*) Sheila, leave them. Come back.

Sheila *enters followed by* **Elizabeth**.

Reggie It was Dad's decision, and as far as I'm concerned that is final.

Tony Well, I'm not accepting it.

Reggie You have no choice. And now if you don't mind I'd like to pack up my bags and leave this house. If that's all right with you.

Tony But it's not fair, you're entitled to half.

Reggie Obviously not.

Tony I don't want your money.

Sheila But . . .

Reggie It's not mine.

Tony I can't live here.

Reggie   Then sell it. I can recommend an excellent solicitor.

Tony   But by rights it . . .

Reggie   Tony, I'm touched by your sudden overwhelming concern for my welfare, but Dad has pointed out his reasons.

Tony   I don't want the money.

Reggie   You won it, remember.

Tony   You let me win.

Sheila   If he wanted us to have it, then . . .

Tony   Shut up!

Sheila   But . . .

Elizabeth   Sheila.

Reggie   I've got his old Bentley, Elizabeth got Mum's jewellery, we're fine. Look if you need a reason, you have a sick child to look after.

Sheila   That's true, Tony.

Tony   She's not sick!

Sheila   Yes, but . . .

Elizabeth   Sheila . . .

Reggie   Well, a child who needs money, anyway.

Tony   I'm doing all right.

Reggie   OK, you're doing all right, but I don't need it. Look, there's a Ferrari and a Mercedes sitting either side of your Rover.

Tony   You bastard.

Reggie   OK, fine, if you want to give me something there is one thing I'd like. I'd like to have this painting.

Tony   Oh, but . . .

Reggie   Too much to ask?

Tony   No, it's just that . . .

Reggie   Forget it.

Sheila   But Tony, it's not even very nice.

Elizabeth   Sheila.

Sheila   Oh, piss off. Stop telling me what to do.

Sheila *exits*.

Elizabeth   Sheila.

Elizabeth *exits*.

Tony   I don't want your charity.

Reggie   I'm not giving you any.

Tony   I'm as good as you are.

Reggie   What's that got to do with it?

Tony   It's not fair.

Reggie   What's fair, then? I buy another place in Spain? I already have more than enough.

Tony   You're entitled to half.

Reggie   So now he's dead I'm entitled to half, am I?

Tony   Yes.

Reggie   Because it's not fair?

Tony   No, because Tom wasn't your dad.

Reggie   What?

Tony   Dad was Dad.

Reggie   Sorry?

Tony   Your real dad. Dad and Bella are your real parents.

Reggie   You know!?

Tony   What?

Reggie   You know?

Tony   You know?

Reggie   Yes, I fucking well know, but until this moment I didn't know that you did.

Tony   You already knew?

Reggie   Oh. It all makes sense now. Of course the constant . . . God. The . . . the . . . You're even more disgusting than I thought you were.

Tony   How come you know?

Reggie   It comes to something when it's your own son who tells you who you are.

Tony   Stephen knows?

Reggie   I'm not being literal! Go downstairs and take a look at him. Does he remind you of anyone? And you knew all the time.

Tony   Well, I didn't . . .

Reggie   Constantly telling me I wasn't kosher when you knew all the while I was. My God, I was more kosher than you.

Tony   You don't understand, I couldn't . . . What d'you mean?

Reggie   And you've spent your whole life taunting me with it.

Tony   What d'you mean, you're more kosher than me?

Reggie   I watched him . . . I mean . . . I refused to . . . see . . . Even his mannerisms are the same.

Tony   Why are you more kosher than me?

Reggie   Oh, me, me, me, me, me, me, me. God. Because both of my parents were born Jewish and only one of yours was. Shall I taunt you with that? Shall I? No. And the reason

I didn't tell you I knew is because Dad, the man you buried in a blue suit who gave you his house, begged me not to. My God. Did you know that all my life I'd been visiting the grave of a man who meant nothing to me?

Tony   I didn't 'know' know, I just sort of knew.

Reggie   And you didn't think you could just sort of share it with me?

Tony   No. Because of Mum.

Reggie   Do you know what it's like to have a big brother? Well, neither do I. You were a mean-spirited, small-minded, nit-picking bully.

Tony   I wasn't.

Reggie   Hiding my toys. Pulling my hair. Sitting on me. Pushing me. Poking me. Stopping me watch television. Messing up my bed. Filling my bath with cold water. Constantly laughing at me. I was supposed to be the annoying one.

Tony   Why didn't you go with Stephen to see West Ham play?

Reggie   What?

Tony   Why didn't you go with him and Dad that day?

Reggie   What day, when?

Tony   When he was given the match ball that you then later lost.

Reggie   I don't know what you're talking about.

Tony   Exactly.

Reggie   Don't tell me how to bring up my son.

Tony   Someone has to.

Reggie   That's rich, you farm yours out . . . Sorry. I shouldn't have said that.

Tony You think that's down to me? If I had my way she'd never have left.

Reggie Tony. Come back. I'm sorry I said that. What's Stephen been saying? Tony?

Tony Some role-model you are. Mr I-Shag-Everything-in-a-'B'-Cup-and-Below.

Reggie Don't you . . . You haven't . . .

Tony Ooo. Scared he won't see you in the perfect light? Dad must be so proud knowing you're following in his footsteps.

Reggie You bastard. If you say anything about . . .

Tony What? Are you going to hit me like you do everyone else? If I had a wife like Elizabeth I wouldn't shag around.

Reggie Look . . . Just . . . Just . . . Look . . . Let's stop this. We obviously hate the sight of each other. It seems we've always hated each other. Just send anything through, anything through that needs sending. I'll sign it and whatever. Whatever needs doing. Send it and I'll sign it.

Tony I'll send it.

Reggie And I'll sign it. Right. Fuck. Fuck.

Silence.

Tony I'm sorry about all that kid-stuff I did. I didn't really know what I was doing.

Reggie And I'm sorry about saying that about Claire, it was crass. I'm sure you've been an excellent father.

Reggie *makes to exit.*

Tony When I was six I saw Dad and your mum together . . . You know, together. I got caught. Dad made me swear not to tell Mum. But I told her. She got angry, slapped me round the face, told me I was a bad boy. She then went into labour too early, and as you know the baby died. They never found out the reason, but I know if it hadn't been for me it would never have happened. It was my fault she died.

Reggie Why was it your fault?

Tony Because I told her.

Reggie You were six.

Tony Yes.

Reggie Oh, come on.

Tony Don't make fun of me. I've just told you something that I've never told anyone, not even Sheila. And then you came along and I hated you.

Silence.

Reggie When I was six I tried to kill you.

Tony Sure.

Reggie I tried to get you to drink a glass of orange juice which I'd half filled with weedkiller. You were babysitting me and you wouldn't let me watch *Blue Peter*, so I went into the shed, found some weedkiller, came back in, mixed it with some orange juice, added a bit of sugar to cover the taste and gave it to you. But you refused to drink it.

Tony You can't have known what you were doing.

Reggie I pretended I didn't, but I think I did.

Tony You tried to kill me?

Reggie Yes.

Tony Would you have let me drink it?

Reggie I don't know. I really don't know.

Tony Thanks, but it doesn't help.

Reggie Last year I came here and had it out with Dad. I couldn't take not knowing for sure, for absolute sure. He didn't offer any resistance, it was like he'd been waiting to be asked. He just broke down and confessed everything.

Begged my forgiveness. Told me he was young and in love and never meant to hurt anyone. Begged me not to tell you. I'd never seen him so weak, it was horrible. I should have thrown my arms around him and said, Dad, it doesn't matter, I love you, I've always loved you, but I couldn't. Here was the man who'd brought me up, who I loved like a god, and I find out he really is my father. It's what I'd always dreamed would be true. I'm too ashamed to tell you how I behaved. I walked out of here just before Christmas and we never spoke a word since and now we never can. That's why he gave you the house.

Tony   He gave me the house because I needed it the most.

Reggie   We're never going to see him again ever . . . ever . . . ever. If only I could have just one more time to say sorry. That's all I want.

Tony   Yes.

Reggie   I just wish . . .

Tony   You can't live your life as if people are going to vanish at any moment. You'd have to spend the whole time constantly telling them you loved them. It'd be exhausting.

Reggie   I guess.

Silence

Tony   What's it like to have a foreskin?

Reggie   Pardon?

Tony   What's it like to have a foreskin?

Reggie   No, I heard you.

Tony   Well?

Reggie   I don't know.

Tony   Well, you've got one.

Reggie   I know I have.

Tony So what's it like?

Reggie I don't know what it's like not to have one . . . What is it like?

Tony I don't know . . . Looks better, I'm told.

Reggie Does it?

Tony Yeah.

Reggie By who?

Tony People . . . women.

Reggie It's not what I've been informed.

Tony Isn't it?

Reggie No.

Tony Oh.

Silence

Reggie How do you . . . er . . .?

Tony What?

Reggie You know. When you're, erm, you know, on your own. How do you . . .?

Tony Oh right. Erm. Well . . . Why? How do you?

Reggie Well, it's easy, isn't it?

Tony Is it? Oh yeah, I suppose it is. I haven't really thought about it. Yeah yeah, that would be better . . . They're not exactly pretty, though, are they?

Reggie Mine is.

Tony Mine isn't.

Reggie That ruins your argument then, though I guess beauty is in the eye of the beholder.

Tony It's a long time since I've managed to get it in the eye of the beholder.

Reggie   Yes. Yes. What was she like, my mum?

Tony   Um. Dunno really.

Reggie   Right.

Tony   Do you think Mum knew?

Reggie   Good question.

Sheila *and* **Elizabeth** *burst in.*

Elizabeth   Sheila. No. Come out.

Sheila   Listen to this. You've got to listen to this.

Elizabeth   Sheila, no. Not now.

Sheila   Listen to this. Oh, I can't. You read it.

Elizabeth   I'm not reading it.

Tony   What is it?

Sheila   We didn't finish reading the will. There's more.

Elizabeth   It's not important, we can read it later, Reggie.

Reggie   What does it say?

Sheila   You read it then. You're the lawyer.

Reggie   What's it say?

Sheila   Read it.

Reggie   'With regards to my funeral arrangements . . .'
Oh no, don't tell me, it's too late now. We should have
found this before.

Sheila   No, carry on.

Reggie   'With regards to my funeral arrangements, this
is going to seem a strange request to you all, but it's how
I should like to go out and be remembered. I have always
thought fondly on my years in the Navy and therefore if
at all possible I should like to be buried at sea.'

*They gradually all collapse in hysterical laughter. As they recover they
become aware of today's whole event.*

Elizabeth We should be getting going. Reggie?

Reggie Yes. Yes we should. Bye, Tony.

Tony Bye.

They shake hands, the women watch.

Reggie Bye, Sheila.

Elizabeth Bye, Tony.

Tony Bye.

Sheila Goodbye, Reggie.

They hug.

Elizabeth I didn't mean what I said earlier.

Tony About me being self-indulgent, self-pitying and whinging.

Elizabeth Um. Yes.

Tony Right.

Reggie You look after yourself, Sheila.

Sheila You too.

Elizabeth Goodbye, Sheila.

Reggie *makes to exit.*

Tony Reggie

Reggie Yes.

Tony I . . .

Reggie I know . . . Let's not leave it so long next time.

Tony No. Let's not.

Reggie *exits.*

Sheila Goodbye, Elizabeth.

Sheila *and* **Elizabeth** *kiss.* **Tony** *sits on the bed and looks at one of the official documents.*

Elizabeth Oh, and I wouldn't sleep next door if I were you, that's where Louis died.

Sheila Did he? Urggh. Thank you.

Elizabeth *exits.*

Sheila Bye . . . Cup of tea?

Tony I'm a bastard.

Sheila Why? What happened?

Tony My birth certificate. Seems I wasn't born when I was born. Or I was born when I wasn't. I'm older than I am.

Sheila Really?

Tony I wasn't born on August the fifteenth, I was born on March the fifteenth.

Sheila No. Well that explains a lot.

Tony Does it?

Sheila You're a Pisces, not a Leo.

Tony I'm a Pisces, not a Leo!?

Sheila You're a fish, not a lion.

Tony Well, that's a relief.

Sheila And it also goes to prove you're not unlucky with birthdays.

Tony No, but I'm a bastard.

Sheila No you're not. A bastard is when you're born out of wedlock. You were born in, just made out. Pretty common back then. Do you want a cup of tea?

Tony Do I want a cup of tea?

Sheila Yes.

Tony I've just found out that I'm half a year older than I . . . it's not my birthday today.

Sheila I'll have that tie back, then.

Tony Is that all you can say? I've been robbed of part of my life. My parents have lied to me . . . again. I'm probably the cause . . . Oh my God.

Sheila What?

Tony Look at that. I've never considered that before.

Sheila What? Look at what?

Tony That's what Reggie was trying to tell me earlier. He knew. Dad must have known.

Sheila Known what?

Tony How could he have known?

Sheila Tony?

Tony Look. His picture. It's obvious – the jaw, the nose, the way the eyebrows are. It's so Reggie.

Sheila Yes.

Tony And so unlike me. That's it.

Sheila That's what?

Tony He's more kosher than me. That's what he said.

Sheila You've lost me.

Tony Mum must have tricked him. Got pregnant by some local waster and bagged the man with the cash.

Sheila Oh, Tony.

Tony That's what happened.

Sheila Don't be stupid. Your mum? Bobbie? The most simple, lovely, innocent person I've ever known.

Tony I'm probably the son of some East End cockle-seller.

Sheila Tony, do shut up, and even if it were true how are you ever going to find out?

Tony I don't know.

Sheila Well, there you are.

Tony Hang on. Hang on. Yes. There you are, or I am. Or not.

Sheila What?

Tony *has picked up his father's old hairbrush.*

Tony DNA. There's still some hair in his hairbrush.

Sheila You've gone mad. I've always suspected it, but now it's proven.

Tony That's what I'm going to do.

Sheila Just ask Reggie.

Tony He'll never tell me, not now.

Sheila And if you're right?

Tony Then I'll know the truth.

Sheila And you'll lose a father because you sure as hell aren't going to trace some eighty-year-old East End cockle-seller . . . What am I doing? I'm actually beginning to seriously discuss this.

Tony Ah, but what if I am right? What if I'm right? What are you doing?

Sheila *is lying on her back attempting to retrieve her lipstick from under the bed.*

Sheila Seeing if I can reach my lipstick.

Tony Sheila! What if I'm right?

Sheila Tony, once upon a time everybody thought the world was flat.

Tony What?

Sheila And most people were happy about it. Didn't even think about it. OK, they maybe didn't want to go too far out to sea in a boat, but most people . . .

Tony I don't see the relevance of . . .

Sheila Well, then they proved it was round.

Tony Yes.

Sheila But they also thought the sun went round us, and again most people were happy, but oh no, some thought, no, it's the other way around.

Tony I'm not following this.

Sheila Now we know that the world is round and we go round the Sun. Or do we? Maybe we're wrong. Maybe they've got it wrong again, but at some point you just have to accept where you are. Accept the truth now, because they'll always be another truth.

Pause

Tony That was very profound.

Sheila I'm not just a pretty face, you know.

Tony But . . .

Sheila But what?

Tony What if it was true or even if it wasn't? They'd never have married if it wasn't for me.

Sheila Maybe. Who knows. Tea?

Tony Yes. I think I've had enough booze for one day.

Sheila I've had enough of everything for one day . . . They both loved you, Tony, to me that was always obvious. The question you have to ask yourself is, did you love them?

Tony Yeah. So what do I do now?

Sheila In what way?

Tony In any way. I don't know what to do now.

Sheila You have a cup of tea and you take me on holiday.

Sheila *makes to leave.*

Tony   Sheila.

Sheila   Yes.

Tony   Very sexy, that dress.

Sheila   Thanks. I like it.

Tony   Fulham are playing on Wednesday. I could get an extra ticket. You, me and Claire could go together.

Sheila   I'm going to sign up for astronomy on Wednesday.

Tony   She doesn't bite, you know.

Sheila   I know . . . OK.

Tony   Really?

Sheila   Really.

Tony   I'm a fish, not a lion.

Sheila   Maybe we're compatible after all.

Tony   Maybe we are.

Sheila   You know, according to Einstein, if we were to get far enough away from here we'd be able to see what really went on.

Tony   I can't take you to the stars, Sheila.

Sheila   I'm not asking for the stars. Lanzarotte 'ould be nice though.

Sheila *exits.* **Tony** *looks at the bracelet and the hairbrush, then crouches down under the bed to retrieve the lipstick for* **Sheila**. *He surveys the room and exits, taking the bracelet with him and leaving the hairbrush behind.*

Fade to black.

Printed in the USA
CPSIA information can be obtained
at www.ICGtesting.com
LVHW020848171024
794056LV00002B/462

9 780413 775122